praise for *five secrets*

"This book is rich with anecdotes and insights that broaden your perspective on life and deepen your commitment to live your very best."
—Brian Tracy, author of *Maximum Achievement, Eat That Frog!* and *Flight Plan*

"Instead of wishing at the end of life 'If I only knew then what I know now' you can know it now! This book has incredible wisdom from people who have real perspective."
—Marshall Goldsmith, author of *What Got You Here Won't Get You There*

"John Izzo has revealed key fundamental truths from our elders, which he has presented in a way that is absorbing and often moving. This is not just another simple meaning-of-life book; it is a carefully researched and edited exploration of a road map to fulfillment for an era that needs it more than ever. The author infuses personal meaning into each chapter, and we feel as though we are going on a personal journey with him. The journey is joyful, heartfelt, often tearful, moving, but always presented with meaning and purpose."
—Janet E. Lapp, Ph.D., psychologist, author, and host of the CBS series *Keep Well*

"Have you ever wanted to sit down with someone who is really wise and ask him or her some fundamental questions about life? How about sitting down with more than 200 wise people? That's what John Izzo did and he offers truths here that you can't afford to ignore. Prepare to be surprised, provoked, encouraged—and changed forever. You will want to keep this book as a constant companion. It is a gentle reminder that it is never too late to live the truths that lead to wisdom, grace, and deep happiness."
—Dr. Kent M. Keith, CEO, The Greenleaf Center for Servant-Leadership, and author of *Anyway: The Paradoxical Commandments*

"John has written a book that takes the obvious and turns it into the essence. When you have finished reading *The Five Secrets* you will find yourself with a new point of view about life. And you will love it!"
—Joel Barker, futurist

"John Izzo is a masterful storyteller. He educates us by weaving a fascinating mosaic of stories that make his point. Let this book be your mentor!"

>—Beverly Kaye, Founder and CEO, Career Systems International
>and co-author of *Love It Don't Leave It: 26 Ways to Get What You
>Want at Work* and *Love 'Em or Lose 'Em: Getting Good People to Stay*

"*The Five Secrets You Must Discover Before You Die* is a magically engaging book: lyrical, poetic, and perceptive. Through deeply moving stories from wise elders, John Izzo masterfully unravels the mystery of what it means to live a full and meaningful life. This book is a joy to read, and it will be an even greater joy to live the profound yet simple lessons revealed in this remarkable book."

>—Jim Kouzes, co-author of *The Leadership Challenge* and
>*A Leader's Legacy*

"I was deeply moved as I savored the wisdom found in *The Five Secrets You Must Discover Before You Die*. This book brings to light much of the lost wisdom of our elders, providing practical ways to live with greater meaning and focus. John Izzo, who courageously puts the word 'die' in the title, offers us profound and simple wisdom for living, for getting to the heart of what it means to be more fully human."

>—David Irvine, author of *Becoming Real: Journey to Authenticity* and
>*The Authentic Leader*

"The things we think we know are usually the things we most need to be helped to remember. This book prompts us to refocus on the principles on which we build the well-lived life."

>—Max Wyman, author of *The Defiant Imagination*

"If you read only one book this year, please make it *The Five Secrets You Must Discover Before You Die*. Dr. Izzo has done a monumental service for all of us in synthesizing fundamental keys to living a happy and meaningful life. This is extraordinary wisdom literature."

>—Larry C. Spears, President Emeritus and Senior Fellow,
>The Greenleaf Center for Servant-Leadership

the
five secrets
you must
discover
before
you die

the
five secrets
you must
discover
before
you die

JOHN IZZO Ph.D.

BERRETT-KOEHLER PUBLISHERS, INC.
San Francisco
a BK Life book

Berrett-Koehler Publishers, Inc.
235 Montgomery Street, Suite 650
San Francisco, CA 94104-2916
Tel: (415) 288-0260; Fax: (415) 362-2512; www.bkconnection.com

Ordering Information

Quantity sales. Special discounts are available on quantity purchases by corporations, associations, and others. For details, contact the "Special Sales Department" at the Berrett-Koehler address above.

Individual sales. Berrett-Koehler publications are available through most bookstores. They can also be ordered directly from Berrett-Koehler: Tel: (800) 929-2929; Fax: (802) 864-7626; www.bkconnection.com

Orders for college textbook/course adoption use. Please contact Berrett-Koehler: Tel: (800) 929-2929; Fax: (802) 864-7626.

Orders by U.S. trade bookstores and wholesalers. Please contact Ingram Publisher Services, Tel: (800) 509-4887; Fax: (800) 838-1149; E-mail: customer .service@ingrampublisherservices.com; or visit www.ingrampublisherservices.com/ Ordering for details about electronic ordering.

Berrett-Koehler and the BK logo are registered trademarks of Berrett-Koehler Publishers, Inc.

Printed in the United States of America

Berrett-Koehler books are printed on long-lasting acid-free paper. When it is available, we choose paper that has been manufactured by environmentally responsible processes. These may include using trees grown in sustainable forests, incorporating recycled paper, minimizing chlorine in bleaching, or recycling the energy produced at the paper mill.

Library of Congress Cataloging-in-Publication Data
Izzo, John B. (John Baptist), 1957–
    The five secrets you must discover before you die / by John Izzo.
        p. cm.
    ISBN 978-1-57675-475-7 (pbk.)
    1. Self-actualization (Psychology)   2. Success.   I. Title.
BF637.S4I99 2008
170'.44—dc22
2007037420
FIRST EDITION
12 11 10 09   15 14 13 12 11 10 9 8 7

designed by detta penna

dedicated to my grandfather,
Henry Turpel,
whose ring I wear and
whose legacy I carry on

contents

acknowledgments

I want to acknowledge several people for their help and assistance in the research for and writing of this book.

This book is based on a TV series I did for the Biography Channel titled *The Five Things You Must Discover before You Die*. If not for the TV series, this research project might never have come to fruition. I want to thank Leslie Sole from Rogers TV who first believed in this project and in the wisdom of my message. Thanks to the entire Rogers/Biography team including Tom, Stan, and Teo, who worked many hours to produce a show I am deeply proud of.

Thanks to Steve Piersanti of Berrett-Koehler for his continuing faith in my gifts as a writer and in the message that this book brings to the world. Steve embodies many of the principles presented in this book, as does Berrett-Koehler, the company he helped create.

Thanks to Ann Matranga whose feedback and editing comments were invaluable in improving the manuscript.

Thanks to my fellow researchers Leslie Knight and Olivia McIvor, who together conducted over 100 interviews. Special thanks to Olivia, who had an incredible belief in the value of these voices and encouraged me to persevere.

Thanks to my able and gifted assistant Elke, who helped immensely with the TV show and this book. You were the glue that kept the "wise elder" project progressing. Your encouragement and belief in this work has always been of great value (not to mention the thousands of ways you assist and push this work forward each and every day).

Special thanks to a few good friends who continue to encourage me and who particularly encouraged this project: Brad Harper, Josh Blair, and Jeff VanderWeilen. Thanks to

Max Wyman, who has become a mentor to me in my mid-life, for which I am deeply grateful. Thanks for my friend Jeremy Ball (also known as JB and CC), who told me that "my whole life had been a preparation to write this book." We are kindred spirits across time and distance.

Thanks to my grandfather, Henry Turpel, whose life has always inspired me and who died before I was able to fully tap his wisdom. It seems to me that I heard his voice in the lives of these special people.

Thanks to the 235 people who took the time to share their life stories with us. I wish I could have included your entire lives in this book. Many of you have become friends and, as you reminded me, friendship matters more than almost anything else. To those who we were not able to quote directly, please know that even if you are not quoted directly, your wisdom has shaped the message of this book.

Most of all, heartfelt love and gratitude to my partner in work and life, Leslie Nolin-Izzo, who produced the TV show and who, I sometimes feel, is the Executive Producer of my life. As always, you challenged me to do it well or not do it at all. Your editing comments for the book and my life have always made things better. You always made my heart dance and still do.

John Izzo

prologue

The prologue of a book is a window from the world of the reader to the inner life of the author. It is a way to answer two questions: Why did the author write this particular book? What will this book offer me as a reader?

I wrote this book because of my lifelong search to discover what it means to live a full and meaningful life. From the time I was a very young boy I wanted to know the secrets to living well and dying happy. The songs I enjoyed, the movies I watched, and the books I read were always about the search for what really matters. More than anything, I hoped that before I died I would figure out what mattered. When I was eight, this search was given a greater sense of urgency when my father died; he was only 36. Life can be short, and we never know how much time we have to discover the secrets to happiness.

Early in my life I had the privilege to spend time with people who were dying and discovered that individuals die very differently. Some people end their lives with deep satisfaction and with few regrets. Others die with bitterness or with sad resignation at the life they might have lived. As a young person in my twenties, I set out to discover what separated these groups of people.

Many years ago now, a middle-aged woman named Margaret told me that she had tried to live her entire life from the perspective of an "old woman sitting on my rocking chair on the porch." She told me that whenever she had a decision to make she would imagine sitting on her porch as an old woman looking back on her life. She would ask that old woman to advise her on the path she should take. It was a beautiful image.

In my mind an idea began to germinate: Could it be that toward the end of life we discover things about life that would have benefited us greatly if we had discovered them sooner? Would we learn some important things about living with purpose and finding deep happiness if we talked to those who had lived most of their lives already and had found happiness and meaning?

Whenever I am going to take a trip, I choose hotels by using a website that taps into the experiences of hundreds of other travelers, people who have stayed there before me. In their candid reviews, I find the "real deal" about these hotels. Over the years I have found many a gem and avoided many a disaster through this simple method. It occurred to me that one could apply this same method to discovering the secrets to living well and dying happy.

I believed that if I could identify people who had found the meaning in life and listened to their stories, the secrets to living well would emerge. Over the last year, I sought to identify several hundred people who had lived a long life and who had found happiness and wisdom, with the goal of interviewing them to discover what they had learned about life.

It seemed to me that most of us know at least one person who has achieved a visible wisdom that others could learn from.

I began by asking 15,000 people across the United States and Canada to send me their recommendations. I asked them: Who are the wise elders in your life? Whom do you know who has lived a long life and has something important to teach us about living? The response was overwhelming. Almost 1,000 names were suggested. Through preinterviews we identified 235 people who represented a diverse group of people who others had identified as wise. My hope was to learn the story of these people's lives and to learn the secrets of life—the secrets we must discover before we die.

The people we interviewed ranged in age from 59–105. They were almost all from North America but were a diverse group in terms of ethnicity, culture, religion, geography, and professional status. Although many of the people we interviewed have achieved great success in their lives, our intent wasn't to seek famous people but rather extraordinary people from all walks of life. From town barbers and teachers, business owners, authors, and homemakers, from priests to poets, from Holocaust survivors to aboriginal chiefs, from Muslims, Hindus, Buddhists, Christians, Jews, and atheists, we sought to answer this question: What must we discover about life before we die? What do those who are nearer to the end of their lives have to teach us about living life?

We conducted one- to three-hour interviews with each of these people. Three of us conducted the interviews: Olivia Mc-Ivor, Leslie Knight, and I. We asked a series of questions that can be found in the final chapter of this book, questions such as: What brought you the greatest happiness? What are your regrets? What mattered and what turned out not to matter? What were the major crossroads that made a difference in how your life turned out? What do you wish you had learned sooner?

The book has four major sections. The first section will help the reader understand the methodology we used and how we selected and later interviewed these people. The second section explores the five secrets that we learned from these 235 wise people. The third section explores how we can put these secrets into practice in our lives; one of the things we learned is that knowing the secrets is not sufficient. Indeed, what separates these people from many others is that they had integrated these secrets into their lives. The final section provides a list of the questions we asked each of these people (questions we hope readers will ask themselves and ask the wise elders in their lives) and a list of the best responses to the question "if you could give only one sentence of advice to those younger than you, on finding a happy and meaningful life, what one sentence would you pass on?" Finally, there is an epilogue discussing how the interviews changed my life.

Writing a book based on the lives of several hundred people presented a real challenge. Each life was unique and offered its own opportunity for learning. Since I believed that presenting the stories of several hundred people's lives might overwhelm the reader, I made the choice to share personal experiences from a much smaller number (about 50) that were representative of the larger sample. I decided to use only first names, and you will find that many individuals appear numerous times, since their lives help to illuminate each of the secrets. Although I share specific stories from this smaller number, the reader should know that, with very few exceptions, the five secrets were common among all those we interviewed. In the chapter titled "The Secret to Life in One Sentence or Less," I share wisdom from a broader number of people.

This is a book for people at every stage of life. It is a book for young people who are just starting out on the journey of life. Just as young internet-savvy people use the "net" to tap the experiences of others with products or travel locations, so

I hope you will find the life experiences of these people equally fascinating. Wisdom does not have to come when we are old; we can find it much sooner.

This is also a book for those in mid-life, like me, who want to ensure that we discover what matters before it is too late. It is also a book for those in their later years, who wish to reflect on their life experiences and discover ways to pass wisdom on to those who follow.

The title of this book was not chosen lightly. *The Five Secrets You Must Discover Before You Die* has two key elements. The first is the idea that there are indeed "secrets" to life. What I discovered in these interviews is that all happy and wise people eventually discover and live these five secrets.

The second element, "before you die," reminds us that there is urgency to discovering what really matters. When I first suggested writing a book with the word "die" in the title, I got a strong reaction from many people. About half said that having the word "die" in a book title was depressing, but the other half said it was "necessary." They said that the word "die" lets the reader know there is an urgency to discovering what really matters in life. In fact, one of the most common things I heard from these people was about how quickly life goes by. We all continue to believe we have forever to discover what we need to . . . but in the end, our time is really quite limited.

Although I had some clear ideas about what I would learn during the interviews, I knew as a researcher that it was critical to keep an open mind. We had to ask the questions, we had to learn about these people's lives, and only then, when we were done, could we step back and ask what common wisdom could be learned from their life reflections. Yet one of the most profound things about what we learned is how clear it all became by the time we finished. In spite of the many differences between these people (age, religion, culture, profession, education, economic status), the secrets to a well-lived human life were common. It seems that what really matters cuts across all the boundaries we often believe separate us from one another, such as religion, race, and status.

All three of us who conducted these interviews were profoundly moved by the experience. Since we did not provide the questions ahead of time, there was often a lengthy pause between asking the questions and hearing answers. Each of us noticed that in that pause we found ourselves reflecting on those same questions. What brought us happiness? What really mattered? When we reach the later stages of our own lives, how will we answer these questions? What will we wish we had learned sooner? It is my hope that while reading this book, you have that same experience. I hope that as you read the stories of these people's lives, you reflect on your own life and begin to discover in a deeper way your own path to fulfillment and wisdom.

There was one piece of personal unfinished business that also compelled me to conduct these interviews. My grandfather was one of the wise elders in my life. Everyone in my family told me that my grandfather was a deeply wise man who had both found happiness and whose life had touched the lives of many other people. My grandfather had three daughters whom he loved dearly, but he always had some regret about not having a son as well. When I was born, my mother said he told her: "John is the son I never had, and I will teach him the secrets to life." My grandfather died of a heart attack when I was only a young boy. I never got to ask him the questions in this book. Yet in the voices of these 235 people, I heard the voice of my grandfather. I know he is smiling wherever he is.

This book has a simple premise: We do not have to wait until we are old to become wise. We can discover life's secrets at any age, and the sooner we discover them, the more fulfilling our life will be.

One of the "wise elders" I interviewed summed up the value of this endeavor. He told me: "If even one person can learn the secrets to happiness even a few years earlier because of what you are doing, it will have been worth it."

So I hope you will enjoy this journey. For me, it was at times joyous, sometimes tearful, and in the end deeply instructive. My conversations with these extraordinary people changed my life, and I hope they will change yours.

why do some people find meaning & die happy?

Why do some people find meaning and die happy? What are the secrets to finding happiness and living wisely? What really matters if we want to live a worthy human life? These are the questions this book seeks to answer.

To live wisely, we must recognize that there are two fundamental truths of a human life. The first is that we have a limited and undefined amount of time—it may be 100 years, it may be 30. The second is that in that limited and undefined amount of time we have an almost unlimited number of choices of how to use our time—the things we choose to focus on and put our energy into—and these choices will ultimately define our lives. When we are born there is no owner's manual provided, and the clock begins ticking the moment we arrive.

We do not like the words "die" and "death." Many human activities are designed to shield us from the truth about life; that it is limited, that at least here in this place, we do not have forever. Some of you may have hesitated to pick up a book with the word "die" in the title, fearing somehow that something bad might happen to you for even recognizing the reality of your own mortality. You may even find yourself a bit uncomfortable as you read these words, wishing I might move on quickly to another topic.

Still, it is the fact that we die and that our time is limited that makes discovering the secrets to life important. If we lived forever, there would be little urgency to discover the true paths to happiness and purpose since given the luxury of eternity we would surely stumble on them sooner or later. This is a luxury we do not have. At whatever age we find ourselves, death sits nearby. When we are young, we may feel that death is a distant and far-off reality, but having conducted memorial services for people of all ages, including a recent friend who died at 33 while traveling in Kenya, I suggest that death is always close at hand, reminding us to get on with life. Derek Walcott, the Nobel-Prize-winning poet from St. Lucia, called time the "evil beloved." On the one hand, we know that time appears evil because it will take from us all that matters to us, at least in this life; on the other hand, time is also "beloved" because it is our very mortality that gives life a sense of urgency and purpose. Our time is limited and must be used wisely.

knowledge versus wisdom

Knowing how to use this one life to its fullest requires wisdom more than knowledge. Wisdom is different and fundamentally more important than knowledge. We live in a time when knowledge (the number of facts) doubles every six months, but wisdom is in short supply. Knowledge is the accumulation of facts, whereas wisdom is the ability to discern what matters and what does not matter. Unless we can discover what really matters, we cannot find true meaning in life.

In my first profession, it was as a minister in the Presbyterian Church. When I was in my twenties I had the privilege of spending a good deal of time with people who were dying. Through those experiences I discovered that individual human beings die very differently. Some people die having lived a life of deep purpose with few regrets. These people come to the end of their lives with a deep sense of having lived a full human life. Others die looking back with bitterness at having missed what really mattered. Even as a young man I realized that some people found the secrets to life and some did not.

Death has never been an abstract concept to me. My father died when he was only 36 years old. He stood up one day at a picnic and that was it. His life had been far from perfect, and now it was over. There would be no do-over. By the time I was 28 years old I had conducted dozens of funeral services and sat with many people in the final days of life. I consider this intimacy with mortality to be a great gift. Maybe because of these experiences, I have always searched for the "secrets" to living a purposeful and fulfilling life. I vowed as a very young person that when my time came, I would not look back in regret for the life I might have lived.

My wife is a nurse by training, and from a young age she too was witness to the reality of our mortality. She worked in the operating room, in a pediatric cancer ward, and in the emergency room. We talk about death regularly. We try to live aware of its presence.

Leslie, my wife, almost died a few times in her life. She was born with a deformed heart and had several major operations beginning when she was a few days old, but three years ago we had an experience that reminded us anew of the fragility of our lives.

She was going into the hospital for a routine and non–life-threatening surgical procedure. To this day I can remember our daughter Sydney, then ten years old, saying: "Mommy, you don't really need to have that surgery, do you?" Leslie reassured her and the next morning was admitted for surgery.

What happened in the next 72 hours is still a blur to me. The surgery went well, she was groggy and then uncomfortable. The kids and I stayed with her at the hospital into that evening. The next day she felt a little better, and I left her room early in the evening so she could rest, telling her that I was going to get some things done at the office and that I'd come visit the next day about noon. We anticipated she would be home within a day.

The next morning I called the hospital around 11 a.m., and my wife was saying things that made no sense, talking to me in sentences that were unintelligible. Rushing to the hospital I soon discovered that in the middle of the night she had experienced a stroke at the age of 37. She was seeing triple and was being transferred to the neuro–intensive-care unit. Later that day, the neurologist asked me to make the hardest decision of my life thus far. "Your wife has had a stroke and we don't know why. We have to make a choice now as to whether to put her on blood-thinning medication. It could save her life, or it could lead to more bleeding, depending on what caused the stroke. The decision is yours." With the information available to me, I decided to authorize the use of the medication. The next several days were tense and frightening.

When something like this happens, we each have our own story. I cannot speak for my wife's experience but the next few months set off a whirlwind of emotions for me. My life was busy and crowded with meetings and tasks. Even while Leslie was recovering at home, I continued to busy myself with these many tasks, and in retrospect I realize that I was not there for her in the way I would like to have been. I kept asking myself: Is this really the right way to live my life? What really matters?

A friend of mine, Jim Kouzes, told me that "adversity introduces us to ourselves," and I was not sure I liked the person I was meeting. While she slowly recovered and I sadly watched her daily struggle to regain the ability to do simple tasks once taken for granted, I struggled to think about the rest of my life. The stroke reminded both of us that life was fragile, but it also served as a wake-up call.

By the time the year was finished, Leslie was mostly back to normal, and I was very thankful. I felt we had been granted a reprieve. But we had been paid a visit. Our belief in the certainty of health and life was shattered by this experience. Life was short. And I began to ask myself: Have I really discovered what matters? If my time came now, could I say I had discovered the secrets to life? Approaching 50, and with my wife recovered from that stroke, I embarked on the journey that I share in this book, a journey to discover "the secrets."

This book emerged from my desire to be clear on what matters, the secrets to a happy, purposeful life. As I have aged, I have found myself asking with a greater sense of urgency the questions that have been there all my life: What matters? What will I be thinking at the end of life? Since I have only so much time remaining, what is the wise use of that time? What are the secrets of happiness and purpose?

the two things we want most

It seems to me that there are two things we want most as human beings. Freud theorized that the primary human drives were to seek pleasure and to avoid pain. As the result of spending my lifetime not with psychiatric patients but meeting thousands of people across many continents and listening to their stories (first as a minister and later leading personal-growth sessions), I believe Freud was wrong, very wrong.

In my experience, the two things humans want most are to find happiness and to find meaning. "Happiness" is often thought of as a frivolous word, as in "don't worry, be happy" (meaning blissfully unaware). We may think of happiness as a temporary state of feeling good brought on by pleasures such as good food and sex.

By "finding happiness" I mean that every human being wants to experience joy and a deep sense of contentment. We want to know that we have lived fully and experienced what it means to be a human being. Joseph Campbell put it this way: "I think that what we're seeking is an experience of being alive, so that our life experiences on the purely physical plane will have resonances within our own innermost being and reality, so that we actually feel the rapture of being alive."*

This does not mean a permanent state of bliss but a day-to-day contentment and joy that create the experience we call happiness. At the end of each day, and at the end of our lives, we want what my grandfather called a "good tired."

But happiness is not enough for us as human beings. I believe we also want to find meaning. If happiness is about the day-to-day experience of contentment and joy, meaning is about the sense that one's life has purpose. Victor Frankl, a student of Freud and a survivor of the Nazi death camps, suggested that the search for meaning is the ultimate human drive. We want, most of all, to know that it mattered we were here, to find a reason for being alive. Some call this a sense of purpose; others might say it is about leaving a legacy or finding a calling. To me, "meaning" is about connection to something outside ourselves. Meaning is about not being alone, because if my life has meaning, it is connected to something and someone beyond the self.

---

*Campbell, Joseph, and Bill Moyers. *The Power of Myth* (New York: Anchor, 1991), p. 52.

Happiness is about the moments of our lives; meaning is about our sense of connection. Perhaps if we were not mortal, happiness would be enough, but our mortality causes us to want to be connected, to know that it matters that we were here.

But how do we discover the secrets of happiness and meaning? How do we find the secrets of living well and dying happy?

Many of us stumble through the journey of living, learning as we go, eventually discovering what matters. Often we discover wisdom when we are old, when most of our life is behind us, when it is too late to act on what we have learned. What if we could discover the secrets of a happy and meaningful life before we are old?

I do not believe we have to wait until we are old to become wise. It seems to me that the secrets to life are all around us, witnessed in the lives of others, those who have found what we seek.

In this book are five secrets we must discover about life before we die. These secrets are the foundation of a fulfilling and purposeful life. They are a gift from those who have lived wisely to those of us who are still climbing the mountain.

are these really secrets?

Why do I call these discoveries "secrets"? Normally we think of secrets as something that few people know, and yet it is quite possible that as you read about the five secrets you may feel as though you were already aware of them. They will certainly not come as a stunning surprise. The dictionary defines a secret as "a formula or plan known only to the initiated or the few." Although you may have heard these things before, what makes these five things secrets is that only a few people seem to live their lives as if they were true. The secret is not that these things are new but rather that they are so universally common among the diverse group of people who others said had found happiness and purpose.

In *Anna Karenina,* Tolstoy writes that "happy families are all alike; but every unhappy family is unhappy in its own way." What I discovered in the interviews is that the happy people had the five secrets in common in terms of how they lived their lives. More importantly, I discovered that these people not only knew these secrets but had put them into practice in their lives.

Knowing the secrets is not sufficient. We all know things that we don't put into practice: exercise is good for us, eating a balanced diet can lead to good health, smoking is bad for our health, relationships matter more than things, and so forth. Yet, many of us live life in daily opposition to the "wisdom" we already have. In this book I seek to answer two questions: What matters—what are the secrets of a fulfilling and purposeful life? How do we put these secrets into practice in our lives and keep ourselves on track? I think of these as knowing and going. Knowing is necessary, but it is not enough.

Before I share the five secrets and the practices to integrate them into our lives, let us examine the method by which I discovered the secrets.

why I talked to the town barber (and 200 other people over 60) about life

> By three methods we may learn wisdom: First, by reflection, which is noblest; second, by experience, which is the bitterest; and third, by imitation, which is easiest.
> ——Confucius

Imagine for a moment that you are planning to take a vacation to an exotic and mysterious country, and you have saved money your entire life to travel there. It is a destination with almost unlimited choices as to how to spend your time, and you know you will not have enough time to explore every opportunity. You are fairly certain that you will never get to take a second trip to this destination; this will be your only opportunity.

Now imagine that someone informs you that several people in your neighborhood have been to that country, explored every corner. Some of them enjoyed the journey and have few regrets; others wish they could take the trip again knowing what they know now. Would you invite them over for dinner, ask them to bring their photographs, listen to their stories, and hear their advice? Although you would filter their experience through own preferences, you would be foolish not to hear their stories.

Life is analogous to this trip experience. We get to take life's journey only once, at least in this form (so far as we know). We have an undefined and limited amount of time, and just as many people wind up regretting the way they took the journey as wind up with a deep sense of purpose and happiness. Why would we not listen to those who have already taken the trip and could tell us what they had learned? The assumption behind this book was simple: If we could identify people who had lived a long life and found happiness, we would discover the *secrets* we must discover before we die.

One of my greatest gifts is that I have always taken an interest in other people. Total strangers will often open up to me about their lives within a short time of meeting me. I believe this is because I have the quality of nonjudgment but also because I believe that we become wise by listening to other's stories. I have heard it said that "wisdom is the reward you get for a lifetime of listening when you'd have preferred to talk."

how we chose these wise people

Perhaps because of my belief that wisdom comes from listening, when I set out to discover the secrets of wisdom and of living a fulfilling, purposeful life, I did so by hearing the stories of others. My method was simple: Begin by asking several thousand people to identify and describe one person who had lived a long life and who they believed had discovered purpose and happiness. I felt strongly that when people find happiness and meaning, those around them notice. Rather than define what purpose means, I believed that if we could find people who had found "it," we could uncover its secrets. It also seemed that if we asked people to identify only one person they knew who had lived long and found meaning, this process would yield a truly unique set of people, and their life stories and reflections could yield the true secrets I sought. Having asked 15,000 people for their suggestions, we were overwhelmed with the response. Each morning our office was flooded with voice messages, e-mails, and letters telling us about parents, friends, and associates who people said had "lived long and found out what mattered." Through preinterviews, we narrowed the list down to just over 400, and after further conversations we ultimately identified 235 people.

Once these people were identified, we interviewed them in person or by telephone for anywhere from one to three hours, seeking to find out what they had learned from living. We asked a series of questions of each person including: What brought happiness? What gave life meaning? What was a waste of time? What would they do differently if they could live again? What were the secrets, and how did they put those secrets to practice in their lives? What were the major crossroads that changed the course of their lives? How did they feel about dying? Most of all we listened to the stories of how their lives had unfolded, the practices that characterized their lives, and tried to read between the experiences to find the secrets.

What is unique about this book is not simply that we talked to so many older people about their lives. What makes it different is that these people were identified by others, usually by people much younger than them, as people who had found happiness and purpose.

When we were young, many of us had wise elders in our lives. Early in my life, like many of you, I encountered wise older people who seemed to know something about life. They may have been grandparents, an aunt or uncle, or a mentor. Likely there was some older person in our life who we sensed had found "it." Somehow, his or her years of living had honed knowledge into wisdom. The facts about living had ceased to be mere knowledge. My grandfather was one of those people. I sensed that he knew something about life, that he had discovered what mattered.

It seems to me that "wise elders" are all around us. All we have to do is look. And these people have much to teach us. The strong bond often found between grandparent and grandchild likely grows from the fact that children often sense intuitively the connection between age and wisdom.

Of course, we also discover early in our lives that not *all* older people are wise. Although wisdom is often associated with age, old age sometimes shows up without wisdom. Many of us know, or have known, older people who are bitter about life and who seem to have learned little from all their years. Knowing this, I talked not just to people who had lived long lives but also with those people in whom others saw the trait of wisdom, which I define as the *capacity to discern what really matters and to incorporate it into your life.*

the value of talking to older people

Talking to older people to find out how to live is not very common in our society. We live in a youth-oriented culture, one that assumes that what is new and current is of most value (whether a laptop, a car, or a person). So why is listening to the voice of elders so valuable? If we are young or middle-aged, why seek older people to discover the secrets? Why did we not talk to people of many different ages who seem to be happy?

There is a Romanian saying: "The house that does not have an old person in it must buy one." There is a reason why human cultures, for thousands of years before our time, revered the old. A lifespan of 75, give or take 20, is not much time to learn wisdom through experience (the bitter route Confucius wrote about).

This past year I had the privilege of spending a significant amount of time with several tribes in Tanzania. It was there among these tribes, where "eldership" is honored, that the idea for this project first occurred to me. In one of these tribes, the Irak (not Iraq) people, a person joins the council of elders at the age of 50. There is one council for men and one for women. All of a person's previous life is preparation to join that council, a group that makes important decisions for the tribe. I met a tribe member who was 49 (my age) and one year away from becoming an elder. He told me it was "better than good" to be on the brink of becoming an elder. One could easily sense how his whole life had been a preparation for that moment.

As tribe members described this process, they asked us: "How does the council of elders work in your society?" We 15 North American men, near and mostly over 50, explained with some trepidation that we did not exactly have a council of elders; that in our society older people were often put into nursing homes or lived lives isolated from the young. We lived in a society that values youth above age.

The elders of this Tanzanian tribe were aghast: How could this be! After conversation among themselves, they strongly advised us to go back home, form a council, and "make those young people listen." For a few bravado moments sitting in the mountains of East Africa we thought this was a great idea. It reminded me that for most of human history, humans naturally recognized that with age, there often comes wisdom worth hearing. I realized this experience was lost in our society.

Interestingly, Irak tribe members did tell us that they often invite younger men and women to join the respective councils, as guests, because some younger people are already wise. What a great lesson. Age often brings wisdom, but we can find it sooner —we can discover the secrets to life at any age.

During this project we had the privilege to interview a number of aboriginal elders. In the aboriginal and native cultures of Canada and the United States, certain older people are called "elders." Unlike the custom among the Irak tribe, age alone does not make a person an elder, and there is no nomination and voting process. Rather, at some point, it becomes obvious that a particular person has found wisdom, and others begin to recognize her or him as an elder. In these cultures, the elders are revered for what can be learned from them. These cultures often honor the spirits of the ancestors for the same reason, for the gift of wisdom they have to impart.

Much cross-generational perspective has been lost in an increasingly urban and mobile society. Years ago I met a boy in Brazil who told me that his best friend was an elderly man on his street. This type of friendship is a gift denied many young people in the so-called developed world, sometimes by society and sometimes by our own unwillingness to listen. As I look back on my life, one of the things I wish is that I had sought the wisdom of those with more life experience than I had rather than always assuming that learning from mistakes was the primary path to wisdom. We desperately need elders in our lives, people who have lived a long time and achieved wisdom.

One of the premises behind my research was a simple assumption: We know wisdom when we see it. A friend of mine, and one of the people we interviewed, has worked extensively with many native ethnic groups in Canada. Some years ago he (who was not an aboriginal) was walking with an aboriginal elder, a small woman barely four feet tall. After a while she looked up at him and said: "You know, if you were in our culture, you would be an elder." This woman had only to walk with my friend Bob, and somehow she knew she was in the presence of wisdom. This story mirrors the process we went through for this book. We asked people to think about their "life's walk" and to tell us the "one" person they would call a "wise elder."

The 235 people we interviewed ranged in age from 59–105. Although they were almost all from North America, they cut across ethnic groups, religions, cultures, three generations, geography, and professional status. From town barbers and teachers to business owners and homemakers, from aboriginal chiefs to artists, we sought answers to these questions: What must we discover about life before we die? What do those who have lived most of their lives have to teach us about living life?

why people over 60?

When we first began the interviews, the magic age was not 60. We began interviewing people over 50. After the first 25 interviews or so, the three of us who were conducting the interviews collaborated. Each of us said that we noticed a big difference between the interviews of those over 60 and those under 60. The best way to describe what we found was that somewhere around 60 we begin to reflect *back* on our lives. It was almost as if those under 60 were still so wrapped up in the experience of living that they could not yet fully step back from it. Over time, however, I began to believe that perhaps something more mysterious and beautiful explained why those over 60 seemed wiser. Perhaps there is a mystical or evolutionary connection between age and wisdom. Perhaps we reflect as we age so that we can pass on what we have learned before we die. What we discovered is that somewhere very close to the age of 60, humans begin to look back on their lives while still living it, which may account for what we call the "wisdom of age." As the poet Czeslaw Milosz wrote: "The peace I felt was a closing of accounts and was connected to the thought of death." Whatever the reason, we all noticed it, and focused our efforts on those over sixty.

This is not to say that there are not many people younger

than 60 who have wisdom. In fact, the premise of this book is that we can discover and live the five secrets at any age. Rather, we felt that talking to people who had the ability to look back on their lives would provide unique perspectives. Besides, sometimes it is not until the end of one's life that one can be certain if one has found happiness. Some people appear very happy and fulfilled at 30 but end up bitterly unhappy, so we felt it was wise to talk to people toward the end of their lives.

When we finished the conversations, what emerged were five clear secrets that we must discover about life before we die. Although our group of interviewees was quite diverse, we found that the five secrets were, significantly, common across many of the boundaries that often separate us—religion, ethnicity, culture, gender, and socioeconomic status. Regarding what really matters and what brings meaning to our lives, there appears to be a common human journey that is not bound by creed or culture.

George Bernard Shaw wrote: "Youth is a wonderful thing; it is a pity it is wasted on the young." I believe he meant that it often takes most of a lifetime to discover how to live and that often our time is almost done by the time we learn what really matters. Yet we need not wait until we are old to discover wisdom, to know what matters—and that is why I invite you to come with me and sit at the feet of the 235 people who showed me the five secrets.

the first secret:
be true to your self

The greatest tragedy in life is to spend your whole life fishing only to discover that it was not fish you were after.
—Henry David Thoreau

Talking to several hundred people about the meaning of their lives was a great gift to me personally and a challenge as well. The stories we heard were profound, interesting, and often poignant. We did not provide the questions ahead of time to the interviewees, so there was a wonderful sense in which the people we were interviewing were often discovering things they knew at a subconscious level while they were speaking. At times it was as though I was witnessing wise people uncovering the secrets of their own happiness. At other times it was obvious that the truths these people were sharing with me were not new to them; they had not only learned these things long ago but had been sharing them with others in some form for many years.

The challenge we faced was finding the common themes in the many stories we heard. People described the same things using very different words. I was reminded of the childhood game whereby a secret is passed down a line of people, each whispering to the next, until the original message is hardly recognizable. I had to listen carefully beyond the particular words and stories to uncover the common core of wisdom.

An obvious question was whether there was one thing that stood out most clearly, one sure secret to contentment and happiness.

I believe there is one such secret, and it is the first thing we must discover about life if we are to live wisely.

There was a set of words and ideas that came up again and again. People kept saying such things as "you have to follow your heart," "you have to be true to your own self," "you have to know who you are and why you are here," and "you have to know what matters to you." What separates those who live well and die happy from most of us is that they continually asked themselves whether they were living the life they wanted to live and following their heart toward the answer. The first secret is to *be true to you, to your self,* and *live with intention.*

choose to live life awake

If we are to follow our hearts and be true to ourselves, we must first make the choice to live our lives awake. But what does it mean to live life awake? Socrates said that the unexamined life is not worth living. There is another way to phrase that: Unless you are *continually examining your life* to make sure it is on target, there is a very good chance that you will wind up living someone else's life, which means coming to the end of your life and realizing that you had followed a path that was not your own.

I learned from these people that wisdom means reflecting more, asking again and again (and again) whether your life is going in the right direction, and making constant adjustments to move closer to the life you desire to live. In contrast to the people we interviewed, many people live completely unreflective lives, simply experiencing and rarely asking how they might move closer to the path they desire.

One woman, a 72-year-old woman named Elsa, summed up the point of reflecting, of being awake. When I asked her to give me one sentence of advice to those younger than her on finding happiness and purpose (a question we asked every person) she said: "I cannot do that. In order to tell a person the secret to happiness I would have to sit down with them, look them deeply in the eyes, find out who they are, find out what their dreams are. I say this because the secret to happiness is to be true to your self." Each of us has a path that is most true to us and if we follow that path, we find happiness. The question that happy people ask is not whether they are focusing on what matters but whether they are focusing on what matters to *them*!

three questions that really matter

But how do we live true to ourselves? The secret is to *live with intention*, to consistently and regularly ask three critical life questions:

- Am I following my heart and being true to my self?
- Is my life focused on the things that really matter to me?
- Am I being the person I want to be in the world?

George was in his seventies and was a retired professor of physics. For almost 40 years he taught young people over several generations, so it was natural for me to ask him what he had noticed about life from teaching those thousands of students. He told me that he noticed "there was a chasm of difference between those students who were following their hearts and those that were not." He told me that some students were following someone else's dream, maybe a parent's, or had simply wandered into a field that was not a good fit for the contours of their truest selves. These students always struggled. But others were "following their hearts, and even if they were not the brightest students, they somehow worked through the challenges. Years later I would meet many of these students, and those who followed their heart continued to do well, while those who had not seemed to struggle their entire lives." Just as Dr. George had noticed in his students, I noticed the same chasm among those I interviewed. When you follow your heart, it makes a world of difference. I saw again and again the consequences of being true to one's self and the bitterness that can overtake us when we fail to do so.

Often the seeds of not being true to our "self" begin very early in our lives, when instead of asking what *we want to do* with our lives *we compare ourselves* to others. One of the people I interviewed, Antony, was an 85-year-old actor who was still directing and performing on a regular basis. For over almost 70 years he had been following the path that he found most true to him: acting and entertaining. Even now his doctor told him "whatever it is you are doing, keep doing it because it is working." Antony told me "all I have done has been to be true to my self."

He told me that when he was very young he was always observing the boys ahead of him in the grades above. Each year he would pick one of them and think "I want to be like him." Then one day he realized that he was not any of those boys. The path to happiness was not in deciding which one he wanted to be like but to determine what was most true to him. "Don't try to be anyone else," he advised, "just make sure you are being you."

Many years ago, a magazine named me "one of the people most likely to become the next Tom Peters." Tom Peters is a business guru best known for his book *In Search of Excellence*.

A few years after the magazine story, I was meeting with some people who were sending me out on a national speaking tour. They asked me to tell them what made me distinctive. I told them about the magazine cover and how I was named the man most likely to become the next Tom Peters! No sooner had I said the words when the CEO of the world's largest public seminar company frowned, saying gruffly: "I don't want you to be the next Tom Peters; there already is one. I want you to be the first John Izzo." I believe he was trying to advise me in the same way Dr. George had counseled his students. The first question must always be this: "Is the life I am living true to my self?" Those words were very helpful to me and guided me to explore more deeply what made me unique rather than trying to imitate others.

is your life missing the mark?

As a young man, I attended a Protestant seminary and studied ancient Greek and Hebrew. In the Bible, the word "sin" comes from an ancient Greek word taken from the sport of archery. The word literally means "to miss the mark," as in your arrow missing the target. The greatest sin is to miss the mark of what you intended your life to be. This is why Wordsworth, the great English poet, could write in *The Prelude* that he must become a poet "else be sinning greatly." In this way, living with intention means asking: How close is my life to the bull's-eye?

There are two levels to this issue of being true to one's self. First, on a day-to-day basis, am I living true to my soul? I like to tell people the problem with life is that it is so daily! A happy, purposeful life is the accumulation of many happy days. What became obvious to me as I was listening to the stories of people's lives is that wise people know what a good day is (a good day for them, that is). My grandfather, who, as I have said, was one of the wise elders in my life, used to talk about having a "good tired" at the end of a given day. He contrasted this with a "bad tired." He told me that a "good tired" was when you lived your life focusing on the things that really mattered to you. A "bad tired" he said often comes even when it looks like we are winning, but we realize that we are not being true to ourselves. It seems to me that the first element of knowing ourselves is figuring out what makes up a "good tired" day for us.

One of the ways we do this is simply by reflecting more. When we have a "good tired" day we take notice of what was true of that day, what were the elements that contributed to contentment. When we have a bad tired day we can reflect on the elements that made the "bad tired."

Having practiced this simple technique for some time, I have noticed several things. On my good tired days I almost always have been outside sometime during the day. Even a 15-minute walk in a park makes a big difference. On my good tired days I have almost always made room for people, especially for friends and family. My work did not feel like tasks; rather, I focused on making a difference in my work, and I had some exercise during the day. By contrast, on bad tired days I focused on tasks all day long—no time for friends or people, no time for reading or learning. By noticing and reflecting on these simple differences, I am able to have more good tired days. This is a pattern I saw again and again among those we interviewed: Happy people know what brings them happiness and consistently make those things a priority.

Most of my life I have played tennis. When I am on a tennis court, I lose track of time, which is not a bad definition of Joseph Campbell's idea of "following your bliss." A few summers ago I attended a tennis camp, and the staff there gave me the following advice. They said that most people don't reflect much at all while they are playing. If they win a point they are euphoric and then frustrated when they lose a point. Most players fail to reflect on why they are winning or why they are losing. The camp taught a simple technique—after every point, ask three questions: Did I win or lose? Why did I win or lose? And what do I want to do differently in the next point based on what I learned? My tennis improved, and so did my life.

Imagine if at the end of every day we asked those three questions: Did today feel like a good or a bad tired day? If it felt good, what were the elements that made it good? If it felt like a bad tired day, what contributed to that feeling? And is there anything I want to do differently tomorrow based on what I noticed today? Imagine if we asked these questions after each week of our life, after each month, and each year. Our life moves closer and closer to our "bullseye."

Of course, following your heart and being true to your self also involve larger questions. Do my career and my work in the world represent my true self? Is my whole life truly my "path"? Am I being the kind of person I want to be in the world?

finding your destiny

One of the people I interviewed, Juana, is a Hispanic woman in her sixties. Her family had emigrated from Nicaragua to the United States when she was only three, as she put it, "literally having come over on the banana boat." She told me about a concept in the Latino culture called *destino*. Similar to our concept of destiny, *destino* concerns the idea that each one of us has a true path that we were born to take. Rather than being fatalistic (as in she was destined to be the president or he was destined to fail), it is more akin to the Sanskrit idea of Dharma, according to which each one of us has a true essence.

Other words have been used to describe this idea, such as "following your bliss," which I mentioned earlier. These are all different ways of saying the same thing—that each one of us has a path most true to us, and when we follow that path we find contentment. But what does it mean to follow our heart and, more importantly, how do we know when we are doing so?

"Following your heart" means many things: It means doing work that suits your deepest interests; being true to your self in the kind of life you choose (and honest about what you want); and taking time to hear the small, inner voice that tells you if you are missing the mark of your deepest desires.

William, 73, is an author, a researcher, and an advisor to people on life transition. He told me that much of his own sense of happiness had come from knowing he was being true to self. "I have found most of my purpose in a sense of destiny. To me destiny is not about the place you end up but the path that you are on. Each of us is born with a path we are meant to follow, not a place we will end up, but rather a certain set of experiences I am meant to have while I am here." He went on and talked about how there had been many times when he experienced strong feelings of being in his destiny, such as when "I was four years old and lying in the grass watching the ants and seeing that they were living on a different scale than I was, and I had this great sense of mystery trying to figure it out. I knew that trying to figure things out was part of my destiny. When I have had such moment the sky did not turn a funny color, but it is just as firm as if it was God-given."

Tom was in his sixties when I interviewed him. He is a Metis native who grew up on the prairie of Western Canada. The Metis are a tribe descended from native people in Canada who married French traders. When he was 13, he had an experience that changed his life. This was not an uncommon experience among the people I interviewed. Many of them could point to a seminal moment in their lives when they recognized who they truly are and why they are here.

As young teenagers, Tom and some of his friends used to love to skate on a large lake on the reservation. In the early days of winter in his fourteenth year, he and some friends headed out for a day of skating. Before they left the village, some of the elders warned them that the lake was not fully frozen, but with the invincibility of youth they ignored the warnings. "We headed out past a place they called Big Island and skated most of the afternoon. I remember on the way out we passed over a large crack in the ice, a crack which appeared each year, so we did not think much of it."

As the daylight started to fade the four teenage boys headed back to the village. When they came to the crack in the ice, Tom's three friends crossed gingerly over the crack, but Tom held back. Yelling to his friends to watch, he skated with all his might and leaped over the crack, but as he landed the ice broke underneath him. Suddenly he was in the frozen lake, beneath the surface of the frigid water. He looked up and swam toward the hole through which he had fallen. Grasping at the ice, he yelled to his friends for help. One by one they tried to come to his aid, but each time he tried to climb up on the ice, it broke apart around him forcing him back into a frigid nightmare.

Weary and shivering, he watched as one by one his friends began to run to the village to seek help. Grasping at the ice one last time, he saw the last of his three friends turn to leave. Tom sank beneath the cold waters. He could feel his life slipping away from him. Looking up he saw only darkness, having lost sight of the hole in the ice.

"I realized I was going to die. For some reason all I could think about in that moment were the trees that lined the lake.

They were aspen trees, and my people called them trembling aspens because they have tiny leaves which flutter in the wind so that the entire forest appears to be trembling. As I began to feel my life slip away, all I could think about were the trembling aspens and how I would never get to see them again. About to give up, I felt the trees calling me and looked up one last time only to find a perfect round hole in the ice that had not been there the moment before. Reaching up I grabbed the ice and it held. I could see my last friend just within earshot and I yelled for him to help. He came back and held out his coat and dragged me to safety."

At the time, he was simply grateful to be alive. Soon after he began to wonder about the experience: "I kept wondering why I thought about the trees as I was dying. Why did I not think about my family, my parents or my grandparents? All I could think about were the trees, these trembling aspens, and that I would not get to see them again. It was a mystery that haunted me for many years."

Almost 20 years later he shared the story with a medicine woman, a healer. She told him that the trees had saved him because it was his *destiny* to lead the ceremonies. In his tribe, the aspen trees were a central part of certain sacred ceremonies. The medicine woman told him: "You were born to be a healer." Tom realized that all of his life he had felt the calling to be a spiritual leader but had resisted the inklings. In that moment he saw his *destina,* his true path. When he became a leader of the ceremonies, he was given his "spiritual" name: White Standing Buffalo. Since that time, for the last 30 years, White Standing Buffalo has found his deepest sense of purpose in leading the dances and being a spiritual guide. He continued to make his living doing other things, but leading the ceremonies, and being a guide to others, became the true source of his meaning.

It seems to me that each one of us has a trembling aspen on the lake of our lives, something that is most true to us. When we heed the sound of these yearnings we find happiness and purpose; when we ignore them we feel a hole in our hearts like the hole in that frozen lake that cannot be filled. We grasp at happiness, and each time it breaks apart in our hands like the thin ice of that frozen lake. For some people, that true path is revealed as it was for Tom in one experience, but for many of us the process of discovering who we are is much more subtle and happens over time.

When I decided to conduct the interviews with people about their lives, one of the people who immediately came to mind in my own life was Bob (who was just shy of 60). In the previous chapter, I related how Bob had worked for many years with aboriginal peoples and that one of the female elders had told him that "if you were one of our people, you would be an elder." He told me it was the greatest compliment he had ever received.

There were many facts I knew about Bob's life, but the interview revealed an inner journey that illustrated what happens when you are true to your self. His mother had been a bird watcher and his father a gardener. When he was a young boy, they gave him two choices for his free time. "They told me I could go outside and play in nature, or I could go upstairs and read books, so I did both. He spent his time wandering out in nature, observing wildlife, especially birds. In his room he read books on nature and birds. From a very young age he felt most at home outdoors. The natural world fascinated him and gave him great joy. When he was about ten, he announced one day to his mother that he was going to "become a biologist," though he admits now that he probably had little idea what a biologist was.

He followed his instincts. Though he has worked in government, in the nonprofit sector and as a volunteer, the common thread has been wilderness. He looks back now with great satisfaction at his lifelong work fighting to preserve wild places. From the beginning it was nature, and being in it, that was his trembling aspen.

Sometimes it can be a gift to see the consequences of not being true to your self early in life. Bob's father had been a respected anesthesiologist, and when Bob was in his twenties, the hospital had a celebration for his father's 20,000th anesthesiology procedure. On the way home from the party, Bob asked his father what it was like to celebrate all those years of being a physician. His father replied: "I would rather have been an accountant. You know, son, what I enjoyed most about being a doctor was keeping my own books." It was a great shock to learn that his father had *not followed his heart*. He spent his days practicing medicine, but it was in keeping the financial books of his practice where he lost track of time. "I decided in that moment that if someone asked me what I felt about being an X, I would not say I would rather have . . ." This image haunted Bob, and he has stayed true to his pledge.

His life also illustrates the importance of knowing one's self beyond choice of career, of how this idea of living with intention and knowing one's self is such an important secret. For many years I wondered why Bob and Mary had no children, but out of politeness I never asked about it. It occurred to me that perhaps a medical problem had made having children an impossibility, and I did not wish to inflict any unnecessary emotional pain on them. When I interviewed Bob he said: "Mary and I are childless by choice, you know. Early in our relationship I told her that if we had children she would be on her own. My path was my work, and I did not want children to impede the work I knew I was called to do, which was protecting nature. Mary felt the same way, and we made that choice together."

Prescriptions for a happy life, when they involve some prescribed elements necessary for happiness, are rarely useful. I interviewed people who were called to be mothers or fathers; this was their truest path, and following that path had made them very happy. My wife Leslie is one of those people; she is naturally a caregiver, and both in the family and in her work as a nurse she followed her true path. If she had not had children she would not have been living her *destina*. But for others, like Bob, the opposite was true. Through reflection and listening to the inner voices of his own heart, he knew he was not meant to have children.

The consequence of not following your heart can be devastating for others as well as for you. One of my best friends had always sensed that his mother found her children to be a great annoyance. She tried her best, but parenting didn't come naturally. Even as a young boy he picked up on the resistance she seemed to have to her parental role. As a child it made him feel unloved. He also knew that his parents' relationship had not been one of great love. His father had a drinking problem.

When he was in his late thirties, he went to visit his mother. Now with the eyes of an adult, he could see the deep sorrow she carried. A stale bitterness pervaded her view on life. With courage and compassion he said to her: "Mom, you never wanted children did you?" After some minutes of silence she said: "Son, there are two big mistakes I made in my life. The first was leaving Scotland. I loved Scotland. The second was marrying your father and having children." My friend's heart was not filled with anger but with a strange mixture of relief and great compassion. The relief was from the realization that his instincts had been correct. There was nothing he could have done to earn a greater share of his mother's affection; it had nothing to do with him. He also experienced compassion. Suddenly he felt empathy for his mother, who had not followed her heart, and for his father, whose drinking had perhaps arisen, in part, from decades of living with a woman who had married him not by following her heart but by hearing the voices of obligation. However, for every person who had children when it was not his or her passion, there is someone who devoted a life to career when having a child would have been an important part of being true to self.

following our hearts requires courage

Following our hearts may involve quieting other voices that may want us to follow their dream. Ron, who was in his seventies when we met, had grown up in a family in which medicine was the profession of choice. His uncle had been a respected physician in the community, and when Ron decided to go into medicine, family and friends applauded his decision. Just before he was about to enter medical school he went to see a gifted chiropractor as a patient. During treatment, he became acquainted with a discipline that believed in the power of the body to heal itself. It affirmed the value of touch, which he intuitively found appealing. "I felt an immediate attraction to this profession, and knew that it fit the contours of my soul. I knew I would be following my heart to do this. But chiropractic medicine was a bit of a mystery to people at the time, so when I announced my intention, my friends let me have it. They said 'so you are going to become a quack now?' But I knew it was my path so I had to crowd out those voices."

Being true to our self often involves hearing the one voice that calls us, even if others cannot hear it. Ron went on to tell me that, later in life when he gave up his successful chiropractic career to become a "healer of energies," he met the same kind of resistance. Again, he knew it was his path. "All of my life I have known what to do. I think it is that way for most people, they know but have to have the courage to act." He also told me that there were two keys to following your heart—*having the discipline to listen and the courage to follow.*

Hearing Ron's story made me think of my own path. I began my career as a minister and wandered into the corporate world when I left the parish. The decision to enter the world of business was not fully intentional. In need of work, and having become fascinated with the role work played in people's lives, I entered the field of management development and found I had an aptitude for it. Yet during the next decade, something was missing. I had entered the ministry, in part, because of a desire to talk to people about the meaning of their lives and about the pressing issues of our time (peace, ecology, and so on). Over time, business was less and less interesting to me, even though it provided a great income and even though I was doing worthy work. It is not that my corporate work was not rewarding, it was and still is, but I wanted to write and speak about deeper things as well. There were so many voices asking me to be practical, encouraging me to go deeper into management development work. Yet I kept hearing the voice that had been there all my life, the one that caused me to choose ministry as my first profession. I knew the truest path for me was to explore issues of meaning and wisdom.

More and more I began integrating issues of personal meaning, loving relationships, and our responsibility to future generations into my work with companies. Not only did my outward success grow, but, more importantly, my sense of being true to my self brought me a deeper satisfaction.

It is part of what brought me to this project. And, as I suspected, somehow the issue of whether I would succeed or fail at the effort became less relevant. As my grandfather had said, a "good tired" was when you had been true to self and a "bad tired" could even happen even when it appeared that you were winning.

This situation raises an obvious question. Does following your heart mean overturning your entire life and going in a completely new direction? What I discovered in the interviews is that in some cases we must make a radical shift in our lives to follow our hearts. Ron had to walk away from medical school to become a chiropractor. But more often than not, the people I interviewed made small shifts, and slowly aligned with their true path.

Tom, for example, the man who had fallen through the ice as a teenager, did not give up his "day" job when he realized at 30 that his way in the world was that of healer. He began studying to lead the healing ceremonies and he put more time into this work. To this day, aside from his family, leading the ceremonies is the most important part of his life, even though it has never been the primary way he makes his living. Over the years he simply made the work of healing a larger and more central part of his life.

Jackie, 66, went into banking at an early age and was quite successful. When she was in her forties she attended a team session, and the participants were asked to introduce themselves by saying why they had gone into banking. When Jackie's turn came, the words started: "Well, I have been a banker for 25 years, but I always wanted to be a teacher. Business was my father's passion." The words came out of nowhere and surprised her with their clarity. "It was a shock to me. It was not that I did not enjoy working at the bank, but I always knew that something was missing."

For weeks she considered her options. She had a great career at the bank and a lifestyle built around that work. Instead of quitting, she began to volunteer as a tutor on weekends at a local center for children. After many months of volunteering there she found out that her bank sponsored a local organization to help children with learning challenges. She researched the organization and told her manager that she wanted to be involved in that part of the bank's work. Over time she became the main person at the bank responsible for connecting with the organization, and (on the bank's time) she made three missions over the years to Africa as part of that work. "Because I realized how important teaching was to me, I was able to integrate it into my life while still working there."

Sometimes such decisions are difficult and may gnaw at us for some time. My friend Gus loves photography, but he makes his living as a construction manager. Though he likes his work as a manager, nature photography has been his trembling aspen, much as being a spiritual guide was for White Standing Buffalo. Some day Gus may have to quit construction or perhaps he will simply keep putting more energy into his photography outside work. Maybe he will become a full-time photographer one day, or perhaps photography will always be a significant "hobby," but only by keeping photography central in his life will he find happiness. It is his *destina*.

Thus the secret I learned from interviewing these people is to *never stop asking whether you are following your heart*, whether the life you are living is truly yours. What I learned is that if you keep asking that question, if you keep moving closer to the bull's-eye, you will find contentment. These people kept asking questions, and like sailors tacking in the open sea, they simply kept making small adjustments across a wide landscape, eventually ending up precisely where they intended to be.

Ron, the man who chose to become a chiropractor, put it

this way: "You have to follow your heart, because to deny that is to deny everything. Of course you will make mistakes, you will miss the mark, but if you keep current with your self, you move closer and closer to who you came here to be."

Perhaps being true to our selves is not just about work, or family, or whether we have children, or where we live. It is about whether the "images" and "moments" of our life feel true to us.

One of the people I interviewed told me about a near-death experience that he had during his fifties. Richard, now in his seventies, told me that while undergoing tests at a hospital, he went into cardiac arrest, and his heart stopped for a period of time. He can remember vividly "being outside" his body and watching from above as the doctors and nurses tried to revive him. He could hear the monitor making the flat-line sound and could hear the doctor say "Richard, stay with us, come on stay with us."

"You know I had always heard that when you are dying your whole life passes before your eyes. What I found is that it's not your whole life but images of your life that you see. In that moment I realized that the images of my life felt right, like I had been true to my self. Ever since that moment I have not had any fear of death. I am comforted by those images because what I discovered is that if you feel good about those images you will not be afraid to die."

This, I believe, is what we all hope for—to know that when we come to the end of our life, we have been true to us, to who we are. Listening to Richard, I began to think about my own life. I closed my eyes and tried to imagine the moments that would pass before my consciousness. What would I regret? What would I wish to find among those images that's not there yet?

One of the things we must do to be authentic is to have

the discipline to really listen to our heart. The discipline to listen means setting time aside to ask important questions. What many of these people had in common, these people whom others identified as being wise, was that they took time on a regular basis to reflect on their lives. Yet we get so busy, we hardly even have time to hear the voices of our own souls. My wife and I led such busy lives before she had her stroke: running companies, raising children, watching television, taking trips, earning money, shopping, writing books, calendars always full, and so on. It didn't seem so very busy at the time, but the thing the stroke did most of all was slow us down. And when we slowed down, we started to listen. We began to depend on each other in ways we had never done before and began slowly to let go of things that were not important. Sometimes it is only when we are forced to be quiet that we begin to see things more clearly.

sometimes the universe makes us listen

My friend David was in his thirties when the universe caused him to stop and listen. He was a senior editor at a large business magazine leading a very busy life. Too busy for questions of whether he was living the life he truly wanted to live. Toward the end of his workday, he was sitting at his desk when he felt a pressure in his chest that soon became a mountain resting on him. In the emergency room of the hospital, as he lay connected to monitors, he thought about his life. Quieted now, with no distractions, he asked if he was truly following his heart. He then began to bargain with the universe. He thought about a simple question: If I live through this night what must change?

He asked a nurse for a pencil and some paper not knowing what the next 24 hours would hold. With Zen-like clarity he wrote down five things:

- Play more

- Adopt a child

- Give back

- More time with family

- Start a foundation

"As I lay there that night, my life passed before my eyes. I did not think that my whole life had been wrong, but I knew there were some significant ways that I was not listening to my heart."

David did not die that night in the hospital; a few weeks later he called me up and said: "The good news is that I'm not dead; the bad news is that I am alive and have the list!" The universe had put him on his back to reflect and forced on him the discipline to listen. Now he would have to have the courage to act.

What about those five things he had written on that piece of paper? He realized he was working too hard and he needed more time for enjoyment. He realized his dream of adopting a child was too important to put off. He realized that he wanted to spend more time with his family. He did not even know where the words "start a foundation" had come from. For the next two years he carried the list around with him. He adopted a son. He played a great deal more. He moved closer to family, and sure enough two years later he started a foundation in his father's name.

Of course, we do not have to wait for an illness to create a list we could make any day of our life. In the native tradition of the Pacific Northwest there is a saying: "Today is a good day to die." What it means, of course, is that today is a good day to live completely. If you were lying on that hospital bed right now, what would be on that short list? To be more true to my self, I must . . .

George, the 71-year-old physics professor who told me that he noticed a "chasm" of difference between the students who followed their heart and those who did not, gave me one more piece of professorial advice. "I always told my students on the first day of class: Don't count on cramming. Don't count on coming to the end of the semester and trying to cram in months of work, it just won't happen. Life is like that. So many people keep saying someday they will follow their heart, be the person they want to be in the world. If there is something you need to do, get to it. If you follow your heart and stay current with your self, it works out."

That is the first secret: *Be true to your self.*

Here are four questions to think about each week to help you live this secret:

- Did this week or day feel like my kind of week/day? What would make tomorrow or next week feel more true?

- Was I the kind of person I want to be this week? In what way do I want to be more like the kind of person I want to be tomorrow or next week?

- Am I following my heart right now? What would it mean for me to really follow my heart right now?

- How do I want to live this secret more deeply next week?

the second secret: leave no regrets

To conquer fear is the beginning of wisdom.
—Bertrand Russell

The bitterest tears shed over graves are for words left unsaid and deeds left undone.
—Harriet Beecher Stowe

What is the one thing we will NOT regret at the end of our lives? I am not sure how I would have answered this question before having these conversations, but I am certain that now I would answer differently.

Regret is possibly the one thing we all fear the most; that we might look back on our lives and wish we had done things differently. In my experience from the last 30 years, validated in these interviews, death is not what we fear the most. When we have lived life fully and done what we hoped to do, we can accept death with grace. What we fear most is not having lived to the fullest extent possible, to come to the end of our life with our final words being "I wish I had."

So, if we want to find true happiness and purpose in life we must embrace the second secret: *leave no regrets*. To leave no regrets we must live with courage, moving toward what we want rather than away from what we fear. To leave no regrets we must overcome the inevitable disappointments that life hands us.

We asked each of our interviewees to tell us about the

major crossroads in their lives, times when they made a decision
to go in one direction or another and how that decision made
all the difference in terms of how their lives turned out. When
they reflected on those crossroads, they almost always noted an
element of risk involved—they had to move toward something
they wanted in spite of fear.

It became evident that at the end of our lives *we will not
regret* risks we took that did not work out as we hoped. Not one
person said they regretted having tried something and failed.
Yet most people said they had not taken enough risks.

Knowing that we will likely regret the things *we did not try*
can have a significant effect on how we make decisions. Failure,
it appears, is not the regret that haunts most people; it is the
choice not to risk failure at all. In fact, many of those I interviewed told me that what we call "mistakes" often turn out to
be the moments of greatest learning.

One way to frame this idea is that *we can never guarantee
success in our lives*, since every attempt at anything holds within
it the possibility of failure. If we love, there is always the risk of
rejection. If we follow a dream, there is always the possibility of
falling short. We cannot guarantee success, but *we can guarantee failure merely by choosing not to try at all*. Choosing to take
a risk, however small, can have far-reaching implications in the
course of a human life.

a life of no regret means risking more

Donald was 84 years old when I interviewed him. A psychologist by training, he looked back on a rich, meaningful life. He
had few regrets. One of the greatest sources of happiness in his
life had been his 56-year marriage to his wife, who had died
six years before our interview. When I asked him about "cross-

roads" moments in his life, he immediately took me back 62 years to a college dance.

"I was a shy young man, very shy, especially when it came to talking to the ladies. In my freshman year at a college dance I saw a beautiful young woman across the room. She was wearing a cream sweater, her hair was soft, and she had a wonderful smile. The moment I laid eyes on her I knew she was the one. This was the woman I was going to marry."

As young Donald looked across that room, he knew she was a popular girl, surrounded by other popular girls, and he knew that popular girls would hardly talk to the shy guys, let alone give them a dance. He knew he risked ridicule and embarrassment if he went up to her and she rejected his offer to dance.

"Taking a big gulp, I walked right over and told her she was the woman I was going to marry. This came as news to her and she wasn't terribly impressed but danced with me anyway. One dance turned to two and then three. Over the next few weeks I had to pursue her quite a bit before she realized this dance would last a lifetime."

Such a small decision, made in his early twenties—the decision to risk failure reaching out for what he wanted—turned out to be one of the most important decisions of Don's entire life. The marriage defined his life in many ways, and even six years after her death he told me "there is not one day that I don't feel her presence around me."

Yet I kept wondering what would have happened if the fear of embarrassment had won out that day; if he had sealed his failure by taking no action? At the age of 84, would he look back and regret not having walked across the room and tried?

Of course, not every small act of courage winds up defining our lives or being a major crossroad in our search for happiness. But since we cannot know in advance the risks that matter, we must always move *toward what we want* rather than *away from what we fear*.

Perhaps we must make a basic choice as to *whether we will live in fear* or *focus on what we want*. Each time we play it safe, we move farther away from our truest self. Each time we choose not to move in the direction of what we want, we plant the seeds of future regret.

One of the most poignant moments in the interviews came when I was talking with a woman named May, in her seventies. She told me how she had been working on six different books for the last several decades. Yet none of them was complete. They sat on her computer in various stages.

When I asked her why she had all these unfinished books, she said: "All of my life I have left things unfinished. I thought it was just procrastination. But as I reflect on it, I believe I have not finished these books because if I ever do finish them I would have to let someone read them. And if I let someone read them, perhaps they will tell me that I cannot write. I suppose it is the fear of rejection that has kept me from finishing."

My heart went out to her. Seventy-one years old, and, because of fear, she might never complete the books that have been inside her all her life. Of course, the rejection she fears could become reality, but it is hard to imagine anything worse than dying with your story trapped inside you.

But many of us do that very thing. *For fear of rejection, or failure, or because we are not sure we can succeed, we die with our book, our dreams, our story inside us.*

When I asked people about regrets and about risk, they often tied the two together. I also began to realize that these people were drawing not only on their own life experience but also on decades of watching how other people's lives had turned out. If you live long enough, you get to observe the lives of many other people, and the secrets to life are revealed in those stories.

Paul, 76, had a successful career in business consulting. He had many friends, had worked in over 70 countries, and had been married for many years. As part of his work he had advised many top executives at a wide variety of companies.

"I worked with a lot of top decision makers for five decades. What I discovered is that the greatest regret at the end of life for many older people is that they did *not* do something, regret at not having taken the chance. People regret what they did not do, even more than what they did. The greatest fear at the end of life is that you played it safe and did not make any mistakes at all."

Ken, the 63-year-old "town barber" of Waukon, Iowa, told me a similar story, not among the corporate elite, but there in the tapestry of a small Midwestern town. "There was a couple in our town. The husband got cancer and died in a fairly short period of time. His wife had all these regrets about not having traveled or done many of the things they talked about wanting to do. This is the great fear of life, that you missed it."

Most telling is that when I asked 200 people what they would want, if they could go back, to tell their younger selves, one of the most common answers was to take more risks. As Craig, who was 60, told me: "What you wish is not that you took more physical risks but more risks of the heart and the risk to truly reach out for what you want in your life."

Many times during the interviews, people identified moments when they took a perceived risk as a significant step on the path to happiness. Juana, in her sixties, told me about the job opportunity that came to her when she was in her fifties. She had always been involved in leadership within the Hispanic community, and when she decided to leave an organization she had worked in for many years (and at the same time leave her home of 27 years), she found herself suddenly "wandering in the desert." Entering the world of leadership development with an organization that reached a broader community felt like a large stretch. She told me: "I had spent my whole life within my own community and had never even been in front of an all-white audience, and suddenly I was a novice." Like so many of the people I interviewed, she credited taking this risk as a major contributor to greater fulfillment. "This stretched me, and now I realize if I had played it safe, there is a whole world that would never have opened up to me." She went on to write books on cross-cultural leadership, which she would likely have never done in the safety of her previous world.

the secret to no regrets

This leaves us with a more important question: How do we take more risks in the direction of what we want? How can we live so as to not regret the steps we did not take?

Perhaps my greatest teacher in this process was a woman in her seventies who had grown up in Germany during World War II. As she looked back on her life, she told me that the most important crossroads were times when she had to act with courage and not fear. For example, after the war, things were very difficult in Germany. At the age of 22, Elsa took the first of many significant risks in her life. She decided to move to Canada and start a new life. At the time, she did not know one person in Canada, she had no job prospects, and did not know the language. She told me that, in retrospect, although the decision felt very risky at the time, it was *the* turning point in her life.

When I asked her how she took important risks, she told

me: "Whenever I had a risk I was considering, I would begin by imagining the highest possible good that could occur by taking that risk. I would imagine all the things that could be true if the risk worked out. Then I would imagine the worst possible thing that could happen if I took the risk. I would ask if I could handle the worst thing, and every time I knew I could handle the worst. Maybe I move to Canada and it does not work out. I wind up broke and alone, and I knew I could always come home. But then I imagined the highest possibility, that I would start a new life; that I would make many friends, find love, and raise children in this new country. Then I held that image in front of me. Whenever I began wavering, I would imagine the greatest good I was striving for. I would always remind myself that walking away from the good that was possible was far worse than the consequences of failure."

Many of us live our lives in quite the opposite way. When faced with a risk, we imagine the worst things that could happen and hold these thoughts in front of us.

Perhaps that is why Don went over to that young woman when he was at that college dance (the popular girl surrounded by popular girls). He knew he could handle ridicule, but he could not handle walking away from the woman he felt he should marry. And May, that woman in her seventies with the six unfinished books; perhaps if she focused on the greatest possible good that could come from finishing a book, the feeling of accomplishment, that image would overcome the fear of failure. From listening to these people I am certain that we can handle the rejection slips on our walls, but lying on our death bed wishing we had finished the books we started, or had taken the trips we always wanted to take—this is truly the worst possibility.

When I was growing up in New York City at the height of the cold war, the threat of nuclear war was very real. I was in second grade when John Kennedy was assassinated. I recall vividly the air raid drills at school. We saw films of nuclear tests and houses blowing up and disappearing. Every few months we practiced air raid drills, preparing for "the bomb's" arrival. To this day, I can remember the fear I felt, that one day I would be sitting at my desk, and life as I knew it would end. When the air raid drill sounded, the teacher would have us all get under our desks. It occurred to me that my old wooden desk attached to the chair would not offer much protection.

One time during a drill, a friend of mine named Kenny walked over to the window while the rest of us cowered under our desks. The teacher said: "What are you doing? Get under your desk!" Kenny responded: "Mrs. Brown, if they are going to get me anyway, I'd rather stand up and watch the bright light than hide under my desk!"

Many of us live our entire lives hiding under the desk, believing that failure and rejection are the worst that can happen to us. Yet these 200 interviews have brought me to a different conclusion, that the thing we *ought to fear most is the regret of having not tried*.

choose the path that makes the best story

How do we keep from living a life with regret? In the introduction to this book I mentioned a woman named Margaret who told me how she tried to live her life from the perspective of an old woman sitting in a rocking chair on the porch. She told me that whenever she had a decision to make she asked herself this question: "When I am an old woman sitting in my rocking chair thinking about my life, what decision will I wish I had made?" She told me that in almost every case, the path she should take became clear to her. Deena Metzger, well-known author and spiritual guide, put it this way: "Choose the path which makes for the best story."

This is an interesting but simple way to live a life with no regrets. We continually look ahead and ask ourselves *when I am old or when I come to the end of my life will I regret the step I am about to make?* Will the way I am living my life now lead to the path of regret or no regrets?

Earlier in my life, as a young adult, I had many opportunities to do interesting things. As I listened to the stories of people's lives, I realized that some of my most significant regrets have to do with the opportunities I turned away, often because of fear. One of these moments occurred while I was in seminary studying for the ministry. On two occasions I was offered a summer chaplaincy internship in two of America's great national parks (Grand Teton and Shenandoah). Nature had always held a special place in my heart, but I grew up in a large city, and I had never had the opportunity to spend a significant amount of time in the outdoors. The idea of working in a park was deeply appealing, and part of me knew that the experience would be invaluable. However, I was involved in a relationship at the time and worried about being separated from this person for a few months, so I turned down the opportunity both times. To this day, I believe that if I had projected my self ahead to the old man on the porch I might have heard my self say: "If the relationship is strong, it will survive the absence, but you love nature and may never be offered this chance again." The relationship did not last, and the opportunity never came again.

There is a more recent example from my life. This past year a good friend of mine offered me the opportunity to spend a month in East Africa with 15 other mid-life men, meeting with tribal elders and camping in the wilderness. This was a dream come true, but it was my busiest time of the year, and

I would have to turn down a significant amount of work to take the trip. This time, I paid a visit to that old man on the porch. He told me: "When you are my age, you won't miss the money you lost this month, but you will carry Africa in your heart." I took the trip, explored several fascinating cultures, saw amazing wilderness that I had never seen before, and missed the presence of my family, which reminded me of how much they mean to me. While in Tanzania, I sat with tribal elders and germinated the idea for this project. My worry about the interference with a "busy" schedule almost got in the way of one of the most important experiences of my life.

The most important thing the conversations that led to this book taught me about this second secret is to make sure we try for the things we want in our lives, because we are unlikely to regret trying and failing. The second most important lesson is that if there is a relationship that must be healed, heal it now. When I asked people about regrets in their lives, most of them spoke about people in their lives, about issues not resolved, words not spoken, broken relationships never healed.

living as if your time is short

Over the years, I have led many personal and leadership development retreats with my dear friend Dr. David Kuhl, a gifted physician and author. During workshops, we conduct an exercise whereby we ask people to imagine that they have only six months to live. We tell them that they cannot be certain whether these will be healthy or difficult months. We then give them a specific date precisely six months from the day of the workshop.

"Pretend," we say "that on that day six months from now, you will die. What are five things you must do before that time?" A tense stillness comes over the room, often covered up with awkward humor. As people begin to write down what they must do in those six months, they most commonly write about relationships that must be healed. Sometimes there is a dream long deferred. Once people have finished their lists, we ask: "If you had only six months left to live and the things on your list are things you must do, are they not important enough to do regardless of how much time you have left?" Left unsaid, but obvious to all, is that we are already in this position. We may indeed have only six months to live, and asking ourselves how we would live our life if we had only that time left is a great path to living with no regrets.

Bob, the 59-year-old biologist, talked to me poignantly about making sure we have no regrets about people. "At one point my parents and I were deeply estranged. They did not approve of my marriage and literally kicked my fiancée and me out of their house, telling me that if I was going to choose her over them I could just get out. For many years we were estranged, but years later I made it a point to have those conversations and work it through. So many people let these things go, and at the end of your life it will haunt you. You have to try at least to work it through."

Lucy, now in her seventies, had been estranged from her mother for many years. They hardly talked for the last 20 years of her mother's life. "I wish I would have reached out to her sooner and tried to show her how to love. I would say to anyone who will listen, if there is something you have to say, say it sooner, even if you don't feel ready."

Many years ago, a woman named Betty attended a retreat I was leading. I spoke about regret and how we often have relationships that must be healed. I asked everyone to write the name of a person from whom they were estranged. Then I asked people to imagine the end of their life; they are sitting on the porch and are very old. What did they wish had occurred with that person?

A few weeks later, I received a letter in the mail from Betty. She told me that her son and she had not talked for almost 20 years. A small hurt had turned, from years of neglect, into a large wound. Neither had spoken or reached out to the other. After my workshop, she thought about being an old woman and decided she would deeply regret not trying to repair that relationship. In her letter to me she said: "I knew that I could live with him rejecting my reaching out, but I could not live with not trying."

She called him and told him how she felt. She said: "I can hardly even remember now what happened between us, and perhaps it was important at the time. I am sorry for my part in it, but 20 years is too long for people who once held each other in their arms." Her son reached back to her with his voice, and years of hurt were set aside. Set aside for each of them as well was almost certain regret at the end of life.

When I asked my friend Bob, now 60, if he were afraid to die, he told me: "I am not nervous about dying. When I go I will have a smile on my face. I feel good about my life, my legacy, and how I have lived my life." This is the reward of a life without regret.

Of course, there is no perfection in this life, and there will be some regrets no matter how carefully we live our lives. Even though some people were identified by others as being the wisest among us, they still expressed many regrets. No matter how well we live our lives, we will always regret something. But still, wise people have showed me how to deal with regret.

regrets are best let go

Many people told me that it was important not to focus on regrets or to be too hard on one's self. John, who was almost 94 when I interviewed him, made some wise observations on the subject of regret. He had spent the first 35 years of his adult life working as a journalist with the communist party in Canada. As a very idealistic young man, having from his early teen years been deeply disturbed by the injustice he saw in the world, he decided to devote his life to working for "the Party," which he, like many others at that time, saw as a vehicle to social justice. Over the years, he saw many reasons to doubt the Party's goals and its methods, but he continued to work in it with the hope that it would change. He saw a glimmer of hope for that change when he had the opportunity to work as an editor for an international communist magazine in Prague. It was 1968, and a reform movement was budding in Czechoslovakia for "socialism with a human face." But that hope was brutally dashed when Russian tanks rolled into that country and crushed the new reform movement. They also crushed John's faith in the Party. For him it was, he says, "the last of many straws." When he returned to Canada soon after, he left the Party.

Yet, he did not allow himself to be crushed by regret, which was a common trait among the people we interviewed. I came to realize that it was not that these people had fewer disappointments or detours than the rest of us, they simply handled them differently. As John told me: "In the first half of my life, the meaning was hoping to achieve a better world, then there was the bitter disillusionment that followed. When that happens, understandably you have regrets and you sometimes wonder: Did I waste my life? I know that I'm richer for the experience, yet sometimes I also wonder what my life would have been like had I taken a different route. But you cannot live your life on an 'if.' I took the rest of my life as it came and had many happy moments. I knew from my childhood years that I had an inherent artistic talent, but my work did not allow me to express itself. While living in Prague for those two years, with more time on my hands, I attended a life-drawing class, and that started a hobby that has given new meaning to the final third of my life. When I came back to Canada, I used my editing skills from all those years with the Party to enter the field of editing in health-care, which I found most rewarding for 15 more years. I also attended classes in all the graphic arts, honed in on watercolors and, after I retired, painting became my third career. If not for these detours, which some might think of as regrets, so many good things might not have happened in my life."

Elsa, in her seventies, told me that the best advice she had ever received was from her daughter who said: "Mom, you just have to dust yourself off and get back up." A common trait among the people whom others had identified as having found happiness was their ability to "dust themselves off and get back up." It is not that they had had fewer disappointments than others did but that they refused to allow setbacks to defeat them. *Perhaps what often determines our happiness in life is the step we take after a setback.* There will always be setbacks, and these setbacks often require us to risk again. To love after we have been hurt or lost. To try even after we have failed or been rejected. Or, as was in the case with John, to simply realize that we have been on the wrong path. John dusted himself off and stepped back into life. Listening to the stories of over 200 people, I realized this was a common thread.

There is a kind of gentle grace that is required from us when it comes to regret. It is often said that we cannot forgive others if we cannot first forgive ourselves. Though one of the secrets is to leave no regrets, most of us will have a few. So we must choose to heal the regrets we do have, to bathe them in forgiveness, to know that in most cases we did the best we knew how to do at the time when we acted. It is a sign of our wisdom that we can embrace regret and let it go. Indeed, one difference I noted between the "wise elders" and the less happy people we interviewed was how they dealt with regret in their lives. The happiest people had come to peace with their lives, whereas un-happy people dwelled on regret and missed opportunities.

However, regret does serve one very important positive function in our lives. Our regrets can remind us of what really matters, and if we listen to our regrets, they can keep us from the deeper pool of regret that may lie ahead. Just as my regret about not working in the national parks helped me say yes to going to Africa, we can visit that older version of ourselves and know what we should do. Our lives can never be without regrets or mistakes, but if we regularly check in with that older version of ourselves we are less likely to leave undone that which we came here to do.

When I asked people I interviewed if they had risked enough, almost every one of them said no. Perhaps after we have lived a long life we begin to realize that there was much less to lose than we thought there was. What chances would you take if you knew you had only one year to live? Are you playing your life safe, hiding under the desk or standing by the window just watching the show? If you look at your life from the per-spective of an old person sitting on a porch—what will you wish you had done?

The second secret is to *leave no regrets.*

Here are four questions to think about each week to help you live this secret:

- Did I act out of fear today or this week? How do I want to be more courageous tomorrow or next week?

- Did I act on my convictions this week? How do I want to act on them more deeply this week?

- What step would I take in my life right now if I were acting with courage, not fear? What might I do differently right now if I were living from the perspective of an old person on the porch looking back at my life?

- How am I responding to the setbacks in my life right now? Am I stepping forward or retreating?

the third secret: become love

> Love is life. And if you miss love, you miss life.
> —Leo Buscaglia
>
> If you want others to be happy, practice compassion.
> If you want to be happy, practice compassion.
> —The Dalai Lama

David, now in his seventies, told me about an experience he had when his father was dying. The family had gathered from many parts of the world to share his father's final days. David noticed that during those last few days his father did not talk about the possessions he had owned. He made no mention of cars, houses, or any other possessions he had acquired during his lifetime. Rather, he surrounded himself with photos of special times from his life—weddings, births, family trips, and times with friends. Watching his father die, David concluded: "At the end of our lives, when we only have a short time left, love is really the only thing we will care about." For many years, David has carried this image with him, an image that has guided how he has lived his life. Leo Buscaglia, the great Italian-American inspirational writer, once said that "life is love, and if you miss love, you miss life."

Our several hundred conversations clearly show that love, both the giving and receiving of it, is the fundamental building block of a happy, purposeful human life. Of course, this realization is not unexpected. When I asked people to guess what

I learned in conversations with older people about their lives, the vast majority of them guessed that love was likely both the greatest source of happiness and the greatest source of regret. They were correct.

Yet, the most important thing I learned about the secrets to a happy and purposeful life was that it is not just the *receiving of love* that matters. I learned that the secret to happiness and purpose is also *to be a loving person.* So the third secret we must discover about life before we die is to *become love.*

love as a choice

When I say we must become love, I must first define love. Love is a word with a great deal of baggage. It is necessary to make a distinction between the *emotion of love* and the *choice to love.* Love is commonly perceived in our society as only an emotion. We say things such as "she is passionately in love with him," that we "love golf and pizza," that we "love to party," and on it goes—but we are referring to the emotion of feeling love. Yet, as I listened to the interviewees, I began to realize that when they spoke of how important love was in their lives, they were defining love more as a choice than an emotion. The secret to a happy and purposeful life was to choose to be a loving person, *to become love.*

Although we may not have the ability to "feel" love at will, we have the power at every moment to choose to become love. We live out this secret in three ways. First we choose to love our selves. Second, we choose to act with love to those closest to us (family, friends, and so on). And finally we must choose to become love in all our interactions.

Paul, 73, was a retired businessman and told me at the very beginning of our interview that he had cancer. He also said he was a volunteer hospice sitter, which meant he spent hours sitting with people in the final stages of terminal illness, helping them to be as comfortable as possible during the dying process. Even though he had a potentially terminal illness, he still spent his days comforting those who were dying.

He told me about an experience he had when he took a shift sitting with a man he had never met before. As he arrived to take his shift, the sitter whom he was replacing pulled him aside. "He told me that the man I was about to sit with had cancer and that the cancer was now in his face. He went on to tell me that his face was quite disfigured and to be prepared, because I may have a reaction when I saw him. As I entered his room and looked at his face, I looked upon a totally deformed face with raw sores. At first, I felt the emotion of disgust."

Paul remembered that, although he was experiencing feelings of disgust, he had the power to choose to love this man. "In that moment, I chose to see him with the eyes of love. His face changed, and I saw the beauty that was within this man. I could see that his spirit brightened because I believe subconsciously he became aware that I had chosen to love him." Paul realized something that many of the people I had interviewed had told me: that the power to choose to love transforms us.

The love that I am referring to is not the emotion of love; *it is the choice to be a loving person.* When I write of the third secret, which is to *become love,* I am writing not about feeling love but about choosing love.

first, love your self

The first way we live this secret is by choosing to love our own selves. Unless we fundamentally choose to see ourselves as worthy, we cannot find happiness. The love of self is fundamental to being a spiritually healthy human being. For some of us, self-love may come naturally because our upbringing and early experiences gave us a deep sense of our own self-worth, but for others the love of the self comes with difficulty.

Elsa, 71, was quoted in the previous chapter on taking risks, but she had the most to teach me about love. Growing up in the midst of World War II in Germany, she had a very difficult childhood. Her father was an officer in the German army. Although she had two older brothers, her father had always wanted a girl, so when Elsa arrived he showered her with love and affection. But her father deserted the family when she was only five, when he chose not to return home after the war. Elsa felt that her mother then began to treat her in an unloving way.

"I remember not feeling very loved by my mother when I was growing up. As a child, it seemed to me that she loved my brothers much more than me. It was not until many years later, as an adult, that I was to find out that it was not my imagination. My father had always wanted a girl, so when I arrived he showered me with love. When he left my mother, she took out her resentment on me. Imagine being a young girl and feeling that your mother did not love you and not knowing why."

Having not received love, Elsa recalls a very difficult adolescence, but she also recalls a moment when she came to an important realization. "At some point, I can't say exactly when, I realized that if I could not get love I had to 'become love.' It is hard to explain, but what I realized was that while I had very little control over whether others loved me, I realized that I had complete control over whether I became a loving person. Somehow I knew that if I became a loving person, people could not help but love me. Also, I realized that God loved me and that just by being a human being I was already completely worthy, and this was something no one could take away from me. Although I cannot fully explain it, there was a transformation when I decided to become love rather than seek love."

Elsa's story reminds us that we have little power over getting love but great power over giving love. No matter how we have been treated by others, the act of becoming love transforms us, illustrated by the lives of people such as Nelson Mandela, who was unjustly imprisoned for several decades but who chose to love. His choice helped to begin the healing transformation of South Africa. History is filled with stories of people who made the opposite choice, of the oppressed becoming the oppressors (whether in nations or in families). What's more, her story reminds us that to become a loving person each of us must begin by acting with love toward our own self.

One of the most important ways we choose to love the self is by being careful what we feed ourselves. They say that we are what we eat, but from a spiritual point of view, we are what we think. Human beings have an average of 45,000–55,000 thoughts per day, a veritable nonstop inner conversation. We all talk to ourselves all day long. Most of our thoughts are benign, but many of them have a large impact on how we see ourselves. For example, every time we tell ourselves things such as "I am a loser," "I am not lovable," "I am unattractive," "I have to prove myself to others," "I am fat," "I am not a good parent," "I am not a good person" we are committing acts that undermine the love of self.

Lee, 78, had spent a lifetime trying to understand the human brain and how we hypnotize ourselves with our own thoughts. He told me: "Often when we are young we get programmed, we get hypnotized with a kind of toxic view of the self. This happened to me as a young person. Through our own thoughts we also have the power to dehypnotize ourselves by choosing to plant flowers or to plant weeds. The subconscious treats every thought as a prayer."

When he said this, I realized that most of the people I was interviewing, the people who had been identified as having found genuine happiness and wisdom, spent most of their time planting flowers. The subconscious does treat every thought as a prayer. These people talked about the power of the thoughts we choose to indulge. Lee called it "planting flowers or weeds." The love of the self is about what we feed our minds. And we have the power over this internal conversation.

One man I interviewed, Pravin, had a father who had severe mental illness and eventually committed suicide. For many years he carried within him a deep sense of responsibility for his father's illness and a sense of unworthiness that came from the fear that he, too, would become mentally ill. It was not until well into his adulthood that he realized that he spent a great deal of his energy trying to prove that he was worthy. He also realized that all day long he planted weeds in his subconscious. Each day he indulged thoughts about being unworthy. But then, through a period of self-reflection, he came to realize that as an adult he had the power to choose to love himself. All day long he could choose not to indulge the thoughts of unworthiness. Whenever he had thoughts that were self-unloving, thoughts about being responsible for his father's illness or that he would become his father, he had the power to replace those thoughts with ones that would lift him up. The change took a great deal of time, but he did in fact dehypnotize himself. And each of us has the power to do this: to replace the unworthy thoughts we have with different thoughts. To replace "I am responsible for my father's illness" with "the illness was no one's fault and I could not have changed it." He had the power to replace "I will become like my father" with "I am not my father and will create my own destiny." At first blush, this approach may seem self-evident and unworthy of discussion, but it is amazing how many of us hypnotize ourselves with thoughts that are self-defeating and how many of us treat our own psyches in an unloving manner.

There is a wonderful story in the Navajo tradition. An old Navajo told his grandson that sometimes he feels there is a fight that is going on inside him. He said it is a fight between two wolves: One wolf is evil. It is the wolf of anger, envy, sorrow, regret, greed, arrogance, self-pity, guilt, resentment, inferiority, superiority, fear of healing my body and mind, fear of succeeding, fear of exploring what has been said by others to be truth, fear of walking in others' moccasins and seeing glimpses of their reality through their eyes and their hearts, using empty excuses that my heart knows to be false. The other wolf is good. It is the wolf of joy, peace, love, hope, serenity, humility, kindness, empathy, caring for those who have helped me even though their efforts have not always been perfect, the willingness to forgive myself and others, and realizing that my destiny is in my hands.

The grandson thought about it and asked: "But grandfather, which wolf wins?" His grandfather replied: "The wolf that I choose to feed."

The first part of this secret is to feed the right wolves within ourselves.

make love a priority

The second part of this secret is to choose to act with love toward those closest to us and to make loving relationships a priority in our lives. When I asked people what the greatest happiness was for them, their first responses almost always referred to spouses, children, parents, and friends. Again and again,

I saw that those people who focus on the development of deep personal relationships in their lives become happy. Conversely, when I asked people about regrets, the first responses were also about relationships as well, either a lack of priority given to them or a feeling of having not acted with love toward those who matter most. Many years ago, as a minister, a bitter older man told me: "I spent most of my life on things. People always came in a distant second in terms of my priorities. Now I realize that my BMW doesn't come to visit me in the nursing home."

One of my favorite interviewees was a 62-year-old man named Ken. He was recommended to me by his son, a hospital executive, as the wisest person he had ever known. I was pleasantly surprised by how many people nominated one of their parents as the wisest person in their life (and I hope one day that my children feel the same way about me). It occurred to me that, as parents, we should strive to live our lives in such a way that our children come to see us as having lived wisely. The son's e-mail told me that "my father is THE town barber in a small Iowa town." The idea of talking to "THE town barber" somehow intrigued me.

Ken had been a barber in the small community of Waukon, Iowa, for 42 years. "There were 13 other barbers in Waukon when I began, but I outlived them all, and that is how I became 'THE' town barber," Ken told me. "I went to all their funerals, and now I cut the hair of their grandchildren."

Being a barber in a small town (Waukon has about 4,000 residents) is akin to being a priest or a minister, except that the profession of barber crosses all affiliations and boundaries. Most people get their hair cut sometimes and for a short time sit in intimate context with another human being, talking and observing. It was obvious from the moment I began talking to Ken that not only did he know a fair amount about living a fulfilling and purposeful life, but he had also been a good student in 42 years of intimate observation. The secrets of what gives life meaning and purpose, and what robs it of them, had not been lost on him.

"You watch long enough, and you figure out what makes people happy," he said. "I noticed that if you have love in your life and a job that gives you purpose, you will be a happy person." It didn't take long to figure out that Ken had both the love of family and friends and a job that gave him a deep sense of purpose, beyond the task of cutting hair. For him, the job had provided the opportunity to serve others and to develop deep friendships.

He told me the best advice he had ever gotten was from his wife's father, who told him very early in their relationship that "there will be uphill battles and downhill ones; it is all part of life. Your checkbook is not your success—the people you meet and influence in your life will be your success."

Ken's father died when he was very young. Since Ken was the oldest of four children, he took on the role of father and decided to make sure he would be a good role model. "I felt I should be the father my own father might have been." He told me that many people had helped his family of four children and a single mother when he was young. And he decided that he would try to be there for people as they had been there for him.

Friends, family, and other people had always been the most important thing in his life. He told his wife that he was going to take an ad out in the paper—"brand new house for sale, never been used"—because they are never home, always out with friends and family.

Ken is a great example of what I discovered in these interviews. If we make loving relationships a priority and if we treat those closest to us with love, we find happiness. That is why the second part of this secret is to make people a priority, to make room for deep friendships, and to make sure each day to ask whether you are acting with love toward those who are close to you.

Of course, it sounds easy to make people a priority and to act with love toward them. What I discovered is that, although this particular secret is not really secret, many people still often put material things before people, and in our busy-ness we forget to act with love toward those closest to us. Many of the deepest regrets people had were about not truly being there for the people they loved.

Dave, 65, a retired bank executive told me a poignant story. When I asked him what was the best piece of advice he had ever received about life he told me: "When I was in my forties, my boss's wife died of cancer. When he came back to work after a few months, he stopped me in the hall one day, grabbing me by the arm. 'Dave,' he pleaded with me, 'spend more time with your wife; spend more time with your wife.' He had no reason to say that to me really; he just stopped me and said that to me. But I believe it was the best piece of advice anyone ever gave me. And if he could see me now, he would probably tell me that I did not heed it."

He went on to tell me that he wished he could go back and place a higher priority on relationships. Although he deeply enjoyed his work, he felt he had sacrificed too much in order to be successful. Dave was typical of many of the people we interviewed. The importance of the people in their lives was often lost in the busy pursuit of career and livelihood.

What's more, people often looked back with regret about having allowed anger or unimportant things get in the way of loving relationships.

Susan, 68, looked back with regret on the relationship she

has had with her adult children. "I was so wrapped up in my own emotional life that I just wasn't there for them in a way that develops the kind of deep bond that some people have with their children. I regret not having really been there for them. I can see that many of my friends have much closer relationships with their adult children, and I wish I could go back and change some things."

Others regretted having put unimportant things ahead of relationship concerns. Don, 84, says he wishes he could go back and talk to his younger self. "I would love to go back and tell my self—Don't get so angry with the kids, they did not deserve it, and most of the time I was angry over such silly things. When my oldest kid was six, he asked me what a psychologist was (my profession). I said a psychologist is someone who tries to make sad people happy." Don told me that a little while later on that same day: "I was giving my three-year-old hell, and he was crying, and my older boy came over and said: 'Dad, what? You are not being a good psychologist'—to which I said, 'right now I am being a father!'

"At the time I did not get it. But if I could go back, I would be with my kids more, the way my wife was there for them. You sometimes forget how important it is to treat those you love with respect."

Moments of my own anger toward those I love, often over trivialities, as well as moments of simply being less than kind to those I love, passed before my eyes. Would I, too, look back wishing I had been more present and more loving? It occurred to me that becoming love to those who matter most to us is often about seeing the larger picture, the love that matters more than things.

A few years ago, when my children were in their early teens, my wife told me that she was buying a used trampoline from our next-door neighbor. It was large and very old (and quite unattractive). Since the neighbor's son had gone off to college, I knew they were eager to offload it. We had just renovated our backyard, and the thought of having that "ugly" thing smack in the middle of our yard irked me. Once it was in place, I expressed my displeasure to my wife. She was unimpressed and told me that I ought to rethink my priorities. I looked out my bedroom window and let out an audible "arghh" at the new view! I let everyone in the family know of my distaste for the new view out my bedroom window.

Hours later I heard the loud laughter of my children bouncing with glee on the new acquisition with their friends. It occurred to me that soon they would be gone and living their own adult lives. Surely I would miss those voices, the echo of hearty laughter, far more than I now missed the beauty of my new "yard." It was an important lesson. In each moment, we must ask what really matters and act accordingly.

John, 93, the man who had left the communist party and later became an artist, had been married for 52 years and said that his marriage gave him the greatest happiness in his life. "Friends were always envious of us," he said, "saying we were lucky to have such a great relationship. When they asked me for the secret, I would tell them that you always have to treat your partner as an equal, which is what we always did. You have to accept each other with the flaws that all of us have, along with the good parts. They might change for the better later, or not, but you have to accept them for who and what they are. Whenever I was angry at my wife, I would ask myself: Is the thing I am angry about more important than our relationship? Is it worth jeopardizing the love we have for each other? And the answer, of course, was always no."

choosing to see others with kindness

In talking with the people I interviewed, I learned the importance of choosing to see those around us with kindness. Some time ago I met an 85-year-old marriage counselor named Maggie. For over 50 years she had been listening to husbands and wives talk about each other, which in itself ought to earn her a good seat in the afterlife. When I asked her what she had noticed in all those years of counseling couples, she told me: "I noticed that when people are first together they focus almost entirely on the things they like about the other person. But over time people focus more and more on the things which irritate them about the other person rather than what they like. If people would just turn that ratio around, most marriages and families would be so much better."

Jim, 86, and still happily married after 65 years, had lived this simple secret. Though he had a great career in the military, when asked what mattered, he kept coming back to the subject of his wife. They met in high school, and he wanted to date her but he was shy. When she broke up with her boyfriend, he took a chance and asked her to go to the movies. New movies cost 25 cents, while the old reruns were 5 cents, but he borrowed 25 cents to impress her. They have been together ever since and eventually married.

Every year for their entire married life he has sent her red roses on the anniversary of *this* first date rather than *their* wedding anniversary. "It is as much for me as it is for her. When I send them every year, it reminds me that through all the ups and downs of marriage, I must never forget why I fell in love with her in the first place." Perhaps each of us must continually look for the "red roses" in those we love, focusing on the things that are good about them.

A study by a major university showed that in the average home the ratio of negative to positive messages is fourteen to one. For every one positive comment we make to a person in the family, we make almost 14 critical comments. A similar study showed that one of the common elements in long-term happy marriages was a seven-to-one positive-to-negative ratio in communication. And it is in our power to change that ratio. At each moment, we can choose to become love and affirm one another. We can choose to see the larger picture.

Jim, now 62, told me about the relationship with his first wife. "My first wife suffered from chronic pain, which surfaced after a surgical procedure, for five or six years. Because of the pain, she struggled with mental illness, and she attempted suicide several times. During that period I never knew if she would be alive when I came home at the end of the day. It was a living hell. This experience made me acutely aware of the importance of personal choice, and I realized that my priorities were family and people first. Even though friends and family, for example, told me that they would understand if I decided that I had to institutionalize her and move on in my life, I did not abandon her. Despite the fact that our life was extremely difficult, by making her my priority I realized the kind of person I was—and I liked that person." He went on to tell me that "when I was young, it was cool work that motivated me, but as life has gone on I have come to realize that friends and family, most especially my second wife and stepson, are the true source of happiness."

It seems to me that Ken, the town barber, was right about his observation about people who sat in his chair all those years: "If you have love in your life, you will be happy." Yet the most important thing I discovered about this secret, to become love, is that when we choose to become love in all the encounters of our lives, when we choose love and kindness as our way in the world, happiness finds us. When we give love away it comes back to us in the form of happiness.

do good if you can, but always do no harm

Bansi, 63, was an immigrant from Tanzania, now living in Canada. Raised as a Hindu, she felt that the choice to be kind was at the center of a happy life. When I asked her about the best piece of advice she had ever received, she told me something her mother told her as a child. "My mother always used to tell me: 'Do good if you can to every person you meet, but always make sure you do no harm.' Living by this simple idea has given me great happiness. Each time I meet someone I try to lift them up in some way by being loving, and then I have made sure to do no harm by what I say or do."

She went on to tell me that each one of us either gives or takes life from others when we meet them. "By what we say and do we can either make someone's day or ruin it. I have always been very careful especially with what I say. The tongue is like a razor; you can do good or cut someone with your words."

It was not long into these interviews when I began to see that the third secret was not simply to get love, or even to give it to those close to you, but to embody love as a way of being throughout your life. By truly becoming love, we ourselves are transformed.

People spoke to me about how, as they moved through their lives, they became increasingly aware of the importance of being a loving person, of the choice to be kind. What I learned is that becoming love not only is good for others, it also transforms us in the process. The more we focus on acting with love, the more we find happiness.

Susan, 68, had been the personal assistant to Cesar Chavez

(the well-known organizer of migrant workers). "The most transforming thing about working with Cesar and the farm workers was discovering the Latino culture. The Latinos were warmer and more open to me than any people I had encountered in my entire life. There was a spirit of giving. It was a culture where relationships and being kind to others was central to life." This experience transformed her as she began to discover that choosing to be kind and loving was the key to happiness.

One reason I came to believe that the choice to become love transforms us is this: Although we have little control over whether we get love, we have almost complete control over whether we become love. The people I spoke to had made a conscious choice to become love in their daily lives, and in the process they found happiness.

Lea, 58, is an African American woman who grew up in the segregated South. As a child, she had known great love from her own community as well as the pain of hatred from outside her community. She told me: "You carry this hatred with you even though you don't realize it. When I moved back to the south when I was in my mid-fifties, I remembered how painful it was to realize you were being judged by the color of your skin. As a young person, I remember when I first realized that there was this difference, that there were certain things that you were not allowed. I remember an experience I had in junior high school. I had attended an all-black elementary school, but our parents decided we would go to this integrated junior high school. My parents prepared us by telling us what we were likely to experience. When we got there the kids were not friendly, and teachers did not think much of you. One day there was a celebration of the town's anniversary, and it was a very hot day watching the parade. We were on a corner, and I got sunstroke and fainted, and I remember there was a drugstore on the corner that did not allow blacks in it. One of the white men went in to get me a Coke—and I remember it so well, we were at the mercy of these people—no power of one's own—I still remember that so vividly. But I also remember that person's choice to act with love."

Lea told me about a morning ritual she has, a time of meditation as she begins her own day. "Each morning I take time for quiet and for reading. Then before I leave the house I say a simple prayer: Lord make me open to love from the time I leave my house until the time I come home. Help me so that when I meet those in my path for whom a kind word, a smile, a thank you might be life changing for them, please do not let me be so busy that I will miss it."

What a beautiful prayer. It is the prayer of those who know this secret, that if we choose to be kind and loving from the moment we wake up until the moment we go to bed each day, something profound happens to us. And when we choose to become love, to be loving to each person we meet, we fulfill one of the core purposes of a human life, to make the world better because we were here.

Abdullah, 87, had grown up as a Muslim in India and lived through the partition in 1948 when Pakistan became a nation. Although he later emigrated to Canada, his childhood memories were vivid. "As a young boy we had Muslim and Hindu friends. But a time came when there was a great deal of violence between Muslims and Hindus in my village. A Hindu boy had been killed by Muslims, and some Hindus came looking for revenge. They tried to take me, but an elderly Hindu man stood between me and them. Of course I was only a boy, so the memories are faint, but I remember his strong arm on my shoulder. He stood his ground and made it clear they would have to kill him to get to me."

For a moment, during our interview, he paused and was silent. Looking down at his hands, I felt he was searching for the right words to find voice. "Love is a difficult word to define, but all of my life this man has defined love for me. He was old. Perhaps he had seen violence and hatred all of his life. Maybe he had simply had enough. But I have always liked to think he was sent to me by the Prophet Muhammad to teach me the meaning of love. It is written in the Koran: 'Do not consider any act of kindness insignificant, even meeting your brother with a cheerful face.' Happiness comes from knowing that kindness is never without meaning. Kindness saved my life."

An old man stood between a small boy and potential violence. In doing so, he entered a chain of events that shaped the future. His love inspired love in another. Listening to Abdullah, I could not help but imagine that elderly man lying on his own deathbed, a faint smile across his weathered face. He had chosen love. His acts of kindness would change the future in ways he would never live to see.

Many years ago, a young woman in her late twenties told me a deeply moving story about her mother that is a great witness to the power of the third secret. She told me about how her mother and father had come to visit. At the end of the visit she took them to the airport, and they boarded their four-hour flight for home. Later that day her father called. "He told me that he had some very bad news. On the flight home my mother had a heart attack as the plane was starting to descend. By the time they landed she was gone. Two days later I had to get on a plane to fly home for my mother's funeral."

She recounted for me the long, sad flight home. As she gazed out at the land passing below her, she could not help but wonder what those final moments were like for her mother.

Was she pleased with her life? Had she died with a deep sense of satisfaction or with regret? Was she afraid or at peace? Did she know how much she was loved? Many times her eyes filled with tears as she tried to catch her breath.

On landing, she headed directly to the funeral home for the visiting hours only to discover a room full of those who had shared her mother's life. Her mother had been a Muslim, but the room was filled with people of many faiths and colors. The room was full of love. Since the daughter had moved away some time ago, she did not know everyone, and she kept asking her father who each person was.

There was one woman sitting alone in the corner. When she asked her father who she was, he said he did not know. After asking some of her mother's closest friends, she soon realized that no one seemed to know the middle-aged stranger sitting alone in the corner. She walked up and sat beside the woman and said: "I am her youngest daughter, and we all have been saying that we do not know who you are, so I am wondering how you knew my mother."

"I am sorry to say that I did not know your mother," the stranger replied.

Perplexed, she asked: "But then why are you here?"

"Many years ago now I was going through a very difficult time in my life. I was so discouraged that I was thinking very seriously about taking my life that day. I happened to be riding a bus into the city and sat down next to a woman who was reading a book. But halfway through the bus ride, she put her book down on her lap and turned to me." The woman continued: "and she said 'you look like a woman who needs to talk.' I don't know why, but she was so kind and so open that I told her what was going on in my life and what I was thinking of doing. When I got home, our time together led me to make a different decision.

And that decision has affected not only my life but the lives of many others."

"But what does this have to do with my mother?" the daughter asked.

"Well, I was so into myself that day that I did not even introduce myself to the woman, did not even know her name. But two days ago I saw her picture in the paper and I came here tonight because I did not know your mother, I did not even know her name. But my 20 minutes with her saved my life."

The young woman cried, and then she smiled. Then she cried again until she was crying and smiling at the same time. She told me that she realized that her mother had lived her entire life that way. Whether it was with her children, her husband, her many friends, or a stranger she would never meet again, love and kindness had been her way in the world. It had made her a very happy woman, and now her daughter saw it had also made a difference in ways she could not have imagined. "My mother's life was all about love, and she brought happiness to others and found it for herself in the process. I said a prayer: Let me live that same life."

Tom, the Metis native and healer who fell through the ice at 13 and found his "destiny," told me this: "What I am doing here today, the choice to love, impacts the whole universe. In our tradition we believe that each act is dispersed for seven generations—my children, my grandchildren, my great grandchildren, and on. Everything we do affects everything else. So when we choose to love, whether our children or a stranger, we change the future."

The third secret is to *become love*.

Here are four questions to think about each week to help you live this secret:

- Did I make room for friends, family, and relationships to-day/this week? Did I allow things to be more important than people?

- Was I kind and loving today/this week to the people clos-est to me? How do I want to be more loving to them tomorrow or this week?

- Did I spread love and kindness in the world today/this week in each interaction? Did I act as if each stranger was someone for whom I could make a difference?

- Which of my wolves did I feed today/this week? Did I spend time with people who lift my spirit? Did I act with love toward my self today/this week? Did I engage in negative self-talk/self-hypnosis? Am I planting flowers or weeds in my self-conscious mind?

the fourth secret:
live the moment

Life lived for tomorrow will always be just a day away
from being realized.
—Leo Buscaglia

Sometimes your joy is the source of your smile, but
sometimes your smile can be the source of your joy.
—Thich Nhat Hanh

If you listen to 200 people talk about their lives, including people who come from races and backgrounds different from your own, you begin to sense the deep common threads of the human journey. Often, people from very different backgrounds use almost identical words to describe their unique human experience.

One of the phrases I heard most often in these 200 conversations was "it all goes by so fast." Elsa, in her seventies, perhaps expressed what many people told me in a variety of ways: "When you are young, 60 years seems like an eternity. But after you have lived it, you realize it is but a moment." We believe we have forever, but soon we realize this is not so.

If life goes by quickly, then one of the secrets to happiness is to get more out of the time we have, to find a way that each moment and each day become great gifts. Thoreau called this "improving the nick of time." Listening to the stories of people's lives, I came to see the fourth secret is to *live the moment.*

At its simplest, *live the moment* means to be fully in every moment of our lives, to not judge our lives but to live fully. It means that we must not focus on the past or the future but experience each moment with gratitude and purpose. It means that we recognize that we have the power in each moment to choose contentment and happiness. As I listened to people, I came to believe that through this secret, *live the moment*, they were telling me to *judge my life less* and *enjoy it more*.

To be honest, all my life I have heard that one of the secrets to happiness is to live in the moment, but I am not sure I knew what it meant until I had these conversations. Living the moment does not simply mean to take each moment as it comes, it means something far more significant. The first thing I learned is that wise people see each day as a great gift.

choosing to be in every moment

Max, a man in his sixties, told me about a man he encounters each day on his walks with his dog. "There is a man I meet when I am walking my dog. He is well into his eighties and still actively involved in a whole variety of things in his life. When I meet him and ask how he is, he always responds in the same way—with a resounding enthusiastic *I'm Here!* I know that what he really means is 'I am grateful to be alive and I recognize what a tremendous gift it is.'"

When he told me about that man, I thought of all the people I have met over the years who, when asked how they are doing, say something like: "Well, I'm here, anyway." Often said with a kind of resigned sadness, what they really mean is "I would rather be somewhere else but I'm here." What I learned in such conversations is that happy people are fully here, wherever they are, whatever they are doing.

Max had been a theater critic for decades and sat through hundreds of performances. He told me about the many performances at which it was hard to be fully present. "Sometimes I would be reviewing a play, and it was so bad that I would think this is an incredible waste of my life. Then I would realize that I was not going to get that two hours of my life back, so I would find something interesting to enjoy in the play. If we want to live fully, we must banish the word BORING from our vocabulary; in each moment we must simply be fully there and take all that moment has to offer."

every day is a gift

One of the things I noticed in these people was a kind of intense gratitude about being alive and a determination not to let even one day go unappreciated. Joel, in his sixties, told me that for many years he had been starting and ending his day with a ritual. "Every morning I wake up and say a little prayer—thank you God for another day. Being a scientist, I am so in awe at existence when I think about this miracle we are living; about me as a conscious entity, here in the Milky Way with this sense and capacity. I ask God to not let me squander this day, but that as I go through my day I will be aware of what a gift it is to live. At the end of the day, before I go to sleep, I recount all the good things that happened, however small, and say thank you for this day."

Seneca, the Roman philosopher, said that "we should count each day as a separate life." Each day is not a step on the way to a destination, it is the destination. We begin to *live the moment* when we recognize the great gift of being alive one more day and choose not to squander that single day, not to ruin it by living in the past or the future.

First we need to make sure that we are *living our life* rather than simply *planning our life*. If we are not careful, we find ourselves forever *getting through things* on our way to what we think will bring us happiness. We may find ourselves continually telling ourselves that we will be *happy if* or that we will be *happy when*. It is not that we should not plan or yearn for things we have not yet achieved or experienced, but rather that happiness is always found when we are able to live in the present moment.

In this regard, my dog has been one of my best teachers. Each day when I am not traveling, my dog Molly and I take a walk up the side of the mountain where we live. For 40 minutes we walk straight up and then walk back down. After taking these walks for several years I came to an interesting realization. My dog was enjoying our walks far more than I was!

For me, the goal was simply to get to the top of the mountain and come back down. The walk was not to be savored but to be gotten through. I was walking in order to get exercise and hopefully to live a longer life rather than seeing the walks as important in themselves. Molly, however, enjoyed our walks immensely. If we encountered another dog, she would stop and greet it. If she saw something interesting, she would stop and explore it fully. She spent most of our walks "smelling the roses" while I spent most of our walks imploring her to "come on, let's get going" on my dutiful march to my goal. She was living the moment, I was getting through it.

After coming to this realization, I committed to taking our walks the way she took them. Since then if we meet a neighbor on our walk, I will often stop and have a good conversation; if I catch a mountain vista or see a beautiful flower, I will stop to enjoy it fully; and if I am lucky enough to run into a friend, I take time to catch up instead of getting to my destination. It has become a metaphor of how I live my life.

living as if it were your last sunset

John, the painter who is 93, talked to me about something he noticed after he turned 90. "I like to tell people that I am almost 94 much as a child might say they are almost eight, because ever since I turned 90 I have this great appreciation for each day."

He talked about mortality and of the limited number of years he had left and how this awareness had begun to shape his daily experience. "When you get to be my age, you are always wondering how long you will live. I have great-granddaughters eight and six, so I wonder, up until what age will I live to see them? Will I see them graduate from elementary school perhaps? I know it is unlikely that I will see them graduate from high school. Now when I see a beautiful sunset or a beautiful performance at the ballet I cry. I cry not only because it is beautiful but because I don't know how many more I will get to see. When you are young, they tell you to be in the moment, but you are not sure what that means. Now I know, and it is true at every age, we never know how many more we are going to get to see, so it is important to appreciate each one and each moment as if it might be your last."

His words reminded me of a line from the film *Prairie Home Companion* when Garrison Keillor's character says "every show's your last show" (and the film indeed turned out to be the final movie directed by Robert Altman). The aging painter's words soon became an important image shaping the moments of my life. Each time I found myself in a moment of joy I began to remind myself that one never knows how many more moments like this will come. Rather than rushing through such moments, I began to practice breathing them in. Occasionally I found that tears came to my eyes in much the way that John had described.

Over the years I have known a number of people who had cancer. One of the most common things you will hear cancer patients say is that when they got the diagnosis, two things happened. On the one hand, time sped up. Suddenly there was a sense that time was speeding by. Yet they will also tell you that time also slowed down. Suddenly each moment and day was treasured and lived more fully. Often for the first time in their lives, nothing was seen as simply something to "get through," and no day was wasted as though it were unimportant. That is why in some support groups, cancer patients refer to the disease as "the gift." Though it would be difficult to imagine gratitude for a potentially terminal illness, it is a gift to become aware that each day is deeply precious and should be lived fully.

Soon after finishing the interviews, I began including a brief time of meditation upon waking up, expressing gratitude for being alive and the hope that I would live the day fully. At the end of the day, I meditate again, expressing gratitude for the good things that have happened to me that day. What I have since noticed is that on those days when I might be tempted to just get through the day, I find myself more present, and even on some of my hardest days I am able to find a place of gratitude.

the present moment is the only moment

The second thing I learned about living in the moment from the people we interviewed is that we must always live in the moment, that the present moment is the only moment in which we have any power. If we are to practice the fourth secret, we must choose to live in the present.

Living in the present means recognizing that we have no power over the past or the future, none at all. The past has already occurred and is behind us. Whatever happened we have no power to change it. Any regrets we had, and any joys, are forever frozen in time. Focusing on the past, especially on regret, has the power only to rob the present moment of its happiness. When we find ourselves in regret about the past we must tell ourselves that we have no power over it, none whatsoever.

But surely we have power over the future? After all, the future has not happened yet. Interestingly, in the present moment we can do nothing about the future either. Think of how much time we spend worrying about the future. Will I get sick? Will something bad happen to the people I love? Will there be a war or a depression? Will my wife leave me? Will my children turn out well? Will my company downsize? Worry about the future has only one real power and that is the power to steal joy. As Leo Buscaglia once said: "Worry never robs tomorrow of its sorrow, but it always robs today of its joy!"

Of course, how we act in the present moment may influence the future, but all we can do in the present moment is to be here fully and to know that when tomorrow comes we will embrace it with the same full energy that we give to the present moment.

Living the moment is easy to say but hard to do. To practice living the moment we must train our minds, often over a number of years. Meditation is great practice for training our minds to be present. The practice of silence and focus of meditation is present in most of the spiritual traditions, including the Christian monastic tradition and Buddhism. When I first learned to meditate, done essentially to clear the mind and put one fully in the present moment, my mind would wander off in all directions—to the past, to the future, to the credit card bills, and to the to-do list. Eventually, through training, my mind became capable of blocking out all these things.

Practice this. The next time you find yourself lost in regret about the past, simply tell your mind: "You cannot do anything about the past, come into the present." If ten minutes later you find yourself doing it again, tell your mind the same thing. Do this also whenever you find yourself worrying about the future. Tell yourself: "You cannot change the future; all you can do is be fully present now, come into the present." Over time, you will find more and more that your mind is fully present in the moment you are in. In that moment you have power, in that moment you can take action.

Self-talk is a serious matter, not taken nearly seriously enough by most people. As I mentioned in the last chapter, each day we have 40,000–60,000 thoughts, and the thoughts that we indulge ultimately shape us. If we allow our thoughts to continually live in the past or the future, either by regretting things or thinking about where we are going instead of where we are, we train our mind to be absent from the present moment.

As I listened to the wise elders, I began to realize that one of the things they had in common, a thing that surprised me and delighted me at the same time, was that they had taken control of their mind; they knew that *we have the power to train our mind*. Most people live their lives with the opposite belief, that somehow our mind is a slave to external circumstances. Rather, I have discovered that happy people know that we are more in control of our minds than most people realize.

Living the moment means we know that at each moment we have the capacity to choose contentment and gratitude. Don, the psychologist who had asked that girl to dance in his first year of college, talked to me about his changing view on the power he had over his own happiness. "Early in life I believed that the external world determined how I felt. I would watch a beautiful sunset and experience great delight. Then when the sun had gone down I wondered, where did that good feeling go? Was it the sun that produced my happiness? I began to realize that the capacity to create that good feeling was within me, not 'out there.' Years later a mentor told me that all I had to do was set my mind aside, and I finally understood."

He shared a simple formula for living life: "I have lived by two principles. One is that if something is worth doing, it is worth doing wholeheartedly—like being here talking to you—or doing dishes—don't do something just to get it out of the way. The second thing is that you have the power to shape your thoughts. It is all in your head."

training our minds for happiness

When Don told me that ultimately your happiness was all "in your head," a light bulb began to flicker. The idea that I could, at any given moment, simply choose contentment and gratitude was radical and potentially life-changing. Don was not telling me that this was easy or that it would not require years of practice, only that it was achievable. What the wise ones were telling me to do was to practice a kind of sweet surrender to life. It was not the surrender of resignation, a mere begrudging acceptance of circumstances; what they were saying was that the power to find happiness was within me, not without. They were telling me that if I practiced, I could choose contentment at any time. Slowly I began a few simple practices: waking up each morning and expressing gratitude, focusing on the good that happened each day before sleep, stopping the incessant worry about the future (and practicing a gentle nudge back to the present moment), and simply practicing breathing in the moments of my life as if they were precious—as if they were numbered. I wish there were some mystical or magical formula to live the moment, but what I learned from these teachers of life is that it takes time and practice to learn this secret.

Many people could remember things their parents or grandparents had told them, things that were lost on them at the time but that they now recognized to be true. Bill, now in his sixties, said that when he and his siblings were young, his mother would come into their room and wake them up by drawing open the curtains and saying "rise and shine, life is what you make it." Bill admitted that "at the time I hated it, but I think it helped me because it was a constant reminder that life was not what happened to you, it was how you reacted to it."

Living the moment means choosing to be in a place of gratitude. These wise elders told us again and again that gratitude was the source of fulfillment. Many of them talked about becoming more and more grateful as they aged and less focused on what they did not have. Gratitude emerged not as a mere attitude but a core "life philosophy."

There was a kind of grace these gifted people had about their lives that I believe to be part of the secret to happiness. They had learned that each day all we can do is our very best. Each day we can wake up and choose to see life as a gift and to be fully present in that day. We cannot always control the outcome, but we can control our reactions. Each day we can bring all we have to that day, choosing to live it fully, seeing it as a great gift. Each day we can train our mind not to obsess on regret, nor to worry for tomorrow but to be in this present moment. Each day we can be grateful for what has happened that day. And we can choose not to judge our lives from moment to moment (am I successful, happy, unhappy, a failure, good, bad) but simply to live our life.

Several years ago, I was giving a talk to a large audience, and there was a young man in his early thirties sitting right in the center of the auditorium in the first row. All through my talk he listened intently. He took a great many notes, he laughed loudly when something was humorous and cried openly when I told a touching story. Occasionally he would nudge his neighbor to listen more intently. After my talk he came up to speak with me, asking if I would sign a copy of one of my books. While I was signing, he thanked me for my "great talk" but I said "no, I want to thank you."

I continued: "You had such great energy, and all through my talk I found myself getting energized just by looking at you. And there you were sitting right in the first row."

"I learned that from my grandmother," he said. "You see, when my grandmother died last year there were no tears of grief at her funeral. There was sadness and there was a great deal of laughter, but when my grandmother died we knew there was nothing she had left off the table. She had taken everything life had to give—every pleasure, every moment fully lived, every day she took all life had to give. And my grandmother had given everything there was to give—every kindness, every day she gave all she had to give to the world. So I learned from watching my grandmother that if you sit in the front row everywhere you are, every day and in every moment, you will die a happy person."

Perhaps each of us should begin our day the way Joel suggested. When we wake up, we say thank you for one more day and ask that we not waste it. When people meet us, we greet them with an enthusiastic "I'm Here," sending a prayer to our subconscious of presence and gratitude. Whenever we find our minds drifting to the regret of yesterday or the worry about tomorrow, we gently bring our mind into the present moment. All during the day, we appreciate each small pleasure, as did John the "almost 94-year-old" painter, because it might be our last. And at the end of the day, we'll recount all the good things that happened, however small, and ask for one more day.

The fourth secret is to *live the moment.*

Here are some questions to think about each week to help you live this secret:

- Did I fully enjoy whatever I was doing this week or day? Was I really "here," or did I just show up?

- Did I take every pleasure that was available to me today/ this week (really smell the flowers), and did I walk with awareness through my life or just run?

- What am I grateful for about today/this week? Did I find myself saying "I would be happy if . . ."? Did I choose contentment and happiness this week?

- Did I live in the present today/this week, or did I let to-morrow or yesterday steal the day's happiness?

the fifth secret:
give more than you take

An individual has not started living until he can rise above the narrow confines of his individualistic concerns to the broader concerns of all humanity.
—Martin Luther King, Jr.

Life is no brief candle to me. It is a sort of splendid torch which I have got hold of for the moment, and I want to make it burn as brightly as I can before handing it on to future generations.
—George Bernard Shaw

Many years ago when I was a young clergyman I conducted a funeral for a man I had not known. I will never forget the day of his funeral as I stood before a closed coffin and gave a eulogy without an audience. Although the man had lived in that county most of his life and although his two adult sons lived only a few hours away, not one person came to celebrate his life. Only the funeral director and I were in attendance. At the time I was only 25, but the experience had a profound effect on me. How, I wondered, could a person live so long and touch so few people?

Later on as I learned more about the man's life, I realized that he had lived a life focused almost entirely on his own needs. For most of his later years he had been extremely bitter, and whatever light he had brought into the world had died with him. His funeral was a symbol of his life; as he lived, so he died.

My own grandfather's funeral was an entirely different experience. When the day came for his funeral, the family was surprised at how many people were in attendance. He had been a quiet man, and yet scores of strangers came up to my mother to tell her what a difference my grandfather had made in their lives. The funeral director apologized for holding the visiting hours in a room "too small for the life my grandfather had obviously lived." At the funeral home, one man told my mother that one day five years ago he was standing outside a dress shop looking at an Easter dress for his daughter, a dress that he could not afford. My grandfather passed by the shop and after a brief conversation insisted on buying it, even though he had little money, and said "pay me back when you can." Scores of people had gathered not because of what my grandfather had taken from the world but because of what he had given.

When we talked to the wise interviewees about their lives, one question we asked was this: "What has given your life the greatest sense of purpose and meaning?" What I discovered in listening to their answers is the fifth and final secret we must discover before we die. The final secret is to *give more than you take*.

ten-minute funerals and ten-hour funerals

People kept telling me that what really mattered most of all in life was what you left behind, that something was different because you were here. The ways people felt their lives had "mattered" varied greatly, but the theme kept recurring. For some people, it was having lived long enough to see that their children had grown into healthy adults who were living loving and useful lives. Others looked back on the good work they had done and how this work would affect the future. For still others, it was simply the knowledge that by giving more than they took in their daily lives, they had somehow stumbled onto happiness. As we listened to these people, whom others had identified as having found happiness, we realized that it is those who give the most who find the greatest joy.

Ken, 64, found happiness in his barber shop in that small Iowa town. For almost 40 years he listened to the stories of those whose hair he had cut and found a way to be of service.

"What I have discovered is the greatest happiness you find in life is always from what you give not what you get. These people who come into my barber shop live hard lives—working the soil. For a half hour, I get to serve them, help them relax, and do something for them. But the best thing about being a barber has been getting involved in people's lives. Being a barber is like being a priest; people come in and tell you about their lives. It might be a teenager having problems with his parents, or a husband having trouble at home. You listen, and in some way you try to help. The greatest pleasure in life is seeing that you make something better."

Ken told me that he attended a great many funerals. He was even called on occasionally to visit the funeral home to give one final haircut. "When you are the town barber in a small town, you pretty much know everyone, so I have attended a great many funerals. What I have noticed is that there are ten-minute funerals and there are ten-hour funerals. Some people live a life that touches so many people in a positive way that people just want to hang around and talk about that person's life. Other people live a more self-focused life and this does not happen. It seems to me you should live your life as if you want a ten-hour funeral."

Listening to Ken, I could not help but imagine my own funeral. Would it be a ten-minute funeral or a ten-hour funeral? Had I lived my life in such a way that others would feel that my life had been a blessing to them? I hesitate to admit that, when I was a young man, I would sometimes imagine what my funeral would be like if I were to die an untimely, youthful death. Filled with ideas of grandeur, I imagined the tears of the bereaved. Now, as a mid-life man, I realize that we don't live our lives so that we can have a nice funeral or memorial service. Rather, we have a nice service because we lived a worthy life. This is what Ken had discovered in his barber shop.

Jack, 67, had studied engineering and reluctantly joined his father's business. He had observed his father's life and saw what a life dedicated to service could bring to a person. "My dad was the greatest role model in my life. He was an unbelievably good guy. He owned a successful company, and yet he started employee ownership in the early 1960s because he believed that it was the right thing to do, long before it was common. He was not very interested in money—he was involved in race relations; almost anyone you asked in a place of a million people—people would say he was one of the most trusted men in Dallas. He worked a lot, he threw the football around. But the greatest gift was just being such a good guy—I admired him, and I could see how much people admired him. I guess that influenced my definition of success."

For several decades, Jack had run one of the most respected private companies in the United States, been on the board of many organizations, and was now head of the school board of a large urban center. When I asked him what had given his life the most meaning he told me: "Well, first my kids and getting that right. If you have kids, I think the price of entry into the human race is to try to leave them better people than you were. You have to pass it off to the next generation. But I am also very proud of our company and the impact we have had on people's lives. I guess I just like making things better."

The more I listened, the more I realized that happy people are always *givers not takers*. They may not have been as selfless as Mother Teresa or Gandhi, but they discovered that the more we give, the more we find happiness.

ask what life expects of you

Victor Frankl was a Jewish psychotherapist who was a prisoner in Nazi concentration camps from 1942–1945. Dr. Frankl later wrote about his experiences in *Man's Search for Ultimate Meaning*. One of the most important sections in the book deals with the issue of suicide.

Frankl discusses the fact that many prisoners at the camps contemplated suicide, which is not surprising given that all of them had been deeply violated, having had their freedom, their livelihoods, their homes, their families, and their dignity taken from them. Frankl noticed that you could not convince someone to stay alive by telling him that he was going to get something from the world, that some happiness awaited him in the future. However, if you could help a person see that the world expected something of him, that there was some good he could do in his lifetime, he would almost always choose life. Frankl concluded that people who know "what the world expects of them will never throw their life away."

One of the reasons that *giving more than we take* is one of the secrets to happiness and purpose is because we have a great deal of control over what we give (but almost none over what we get). Each day, we have the power to give without limit. We can choose kindness, to serve, to love, to be generous, and to leave the world better in some way. I came to believe that there is something in us as human beings that longs to make a contribution while we are here.

Antony, 86, had been an actor his entire life, having appeared both in films and stage productions on several continents, and he was still performing and directing. From the moment we met, it was clear to me that he had lived the five secrets. He had found work he loved and followed his heart. He had made room for love and given love to others. Although he enjoyed applause and the accolades, he told me that what really mattered was seeing how he had influenced people.

"When I was young, it was all about getting the part. But as you get older, you realize that there is little true joy in getting paid to pretend you are ecstatic over a cup of coffee; you want to know your work mattered. Recently I was starring as Morrie in the play *Tuesdays with Morrie*, and the reviews were great. But what meant the most to me was a letter I received from a young man who had attended the show. He was visiting with his family from Korea and wrote to tell me that it was the first play he had ever seen and that my performance had changed his view about life and what really mattered. That letter meant more to me than all the applause."

The 86-year-old actor also reminded me that we often don't realize for many years how our life has made a difference. Antony told me a wonderful story about an experience he had with a former student.

"Earlier in my life, I had taught acting while in England, and although I always enjoyed acting more than teaching, I believe I made a real difference for students. Perhaps it is because I did not try to get them to act MY way but tried to help them discover their own style."

Almost 40 years after moving to Canada, he was returning to England with his wife to do some work and was contacted by a former student. The student asked if he might take them to dinner while they were in London and supplied an address for the meeting. When Antony and his wife arrived they realized it was a very, very expensive gourmet restaurant.

They had a great dinner and good conversation catching up. When the bill arrived, Antony asked to contribute because he knew it was a large tab. But Kenny, his student of more than four decades ago, took the bill himself.

"No, I insist on paying. Don't you realize," the former student now in his fifties said, "that everything I have in my life I owe to you! Your teaching changed my life. You lit a fire in me for acting and taught me what it means to be a professional. Your teaching is what made me a success."

Although he had fond memories of his former pupil, he had had no idea what a difference he had made in this person's life. "I realized then that you never know what a difference you make in people's lives. Often we don't find out for many years and sometimes never. That had such an effect on me to realize that I had made such an impact on his life."

This is true of course for each one of us, not just for Antony. We often see only the tip of the iceberg in terms of the difference we make during our lifetime. Many of those we interviewed told me stories of funerals they had attended for loved ones and how there were so many people who showed up to talk about how this person and that person had made a difference for them. We make a difference, even when we do not know it.

One of the things I came to believe in these interviews is that many of us long for connection to something larger than ourselves. Giving connects us to something larger. George, the 71-year-old physicist, talked to me about his spiritual beliefs. "The more I study physics, the more I believe in how much things are connected. There is a connectedness in the universe we don't fully understand." He went on to tell me that "sooner or later you realize that you are not going to take anything with you but you can leave something behind."

the great task of life: lose yourself

During the time I was conducting these interviews, many people asked me about the role "religion" or "spirituality" played in the lives of those who, others said, had found happiness and purpose. Were these people whom others named as wise and happy more likely to be "religious"? I discovered that what these people had in common wasn't religion in the normal way we identify it but a connection to something larger than them. For some of them, it was belief in a personal God; for others, it was a belief in being connected to the entire human journey (that which comes before and after us), and for still others a strong sense that there was a great mystery to which we are connected as human beings. In all cases, at the heart of this connection was the importance of being of service and of being charitable. Jim put it this way: "What gave my life meaning is knowing that I left the campsite better than I found it."

When Dick, 70, was a teenager he found a deep connection with God. "I asked God into my life and what really made the biggest difference for me has been the Golden Rule, this simple idea of being kind to others. I have tried to live it in my business and my personal life. Over the years it has brought me into some amazing situations. For example, I met a homeless, gray-bearded man in New Orleans. My friend and I were there on business just walking in the French Quarter at night, when this man just came out of the shadows and asked me for food. My friend was shocked when I invited him to join us in a restaurant in the French Quarter. I told him he could eat as much as he liked, and he did. When we left him, he gave me this note of love, just thanking me for being so kind to him. I have kept a diary of all the times I have been able to live out that simple rule of doing unto others. And this has been the greatest happiness."

Donald, 84, had grown up in a household where charity was the basis for a good life. "The idea of service is more a Christian idea; for the Jewish people, it is the concept of charity. When I was a young boy, my parents had boxes they kept by the door. Each night my father would come home and put coins in each of the boxes which represented different charities. They made sure that we knew what each of the boxes was for, so that we understood the needs of those we were helping." Much as the "golden rule" had guided Dick's life, the Jewish concept of Tzedakah, which is the obligation to give to charity generally, and to the poor especially, had shaped Donald's search for happiness.

Yet this feeling of being connected through being of service was not limited to those who had strong religious beliefs. Those who told me clearly they were atheists or agnostics talked about how the connection to something larger was central to finding happiness. Bob, 60, is a biologist, a profession that, as I said earlier, he told his mother he would pursue when he was only ten. His love of the outdoors has been the focus of his life, and he feels a deep connection with wilderness. "When you are a biologist you deal with loss every day as you see the natural world being destroyed."

The feeling that he had made things better gave him a deep sense of purpose. "I can look on a map and know there are green places that will outlive me. I know that I have helped build several strong organizations that also will have a life beyond me. For some people their legacy is their children, for me it was my work."

As I mentioned in the preface, we did interview a few "bitter elders" who slipped into the group of interviewees. That is, although we asked people to give us names of people who had lived a long life and found wisdom, there were a few who turned out to be bitter about the lives they had lived. I noticed that one of the most significant differences between the elders who were content about their lives and those who were bitter was their sense of connection to something larger than self.

One of my conclusions is that there are two great tasks of a human life: to *find ourselves and to lose ourselves.* We find ourselves by discovering our destiny and being true to ourselves. Yet it is not enough to find ourselves, we also must lose ourselves.

The loss of self is about seeing that we are connected to something much larger, something that had a life before us and that will have a life after us. There are many names for this phenomenon in the spiritual traditions, but the common element is the loss of the self as an entity of great significance. We are significant because we are part of a larger entity. For some this is God, for some it is the human journey, and for others all of nature. What I found is that those who both found themselves and lost themselves found happiness. There is no better way to lose ourselves than to dedicate our life to giving, to leaving the world better than we found it. This connects us to the future and links us to the past.

Our connection to the chain of life gives our life meaning. Bill, 64, said: "I get purpose and meaning from my two children as well as my four grandchildren, a sense of meaning beyond my physical self. My children turned out to be really good people who are engaged in caring about other people. Then I look at my own mother at 85, and she is the one who passed those values on to me. There is a great sense of purpose being part of the flow, a chain of love spanning many generations."

One of the most poignant stories I heard was from a man named Harvey, a 63-year-old former businessman who became an actor in his fifties and went on to act in over 50 films. "The most important day of my life is a day I don't even remember. The most important day was the day of my birth because I was lucky enough to be born to wonderful parents (and you don't get much luckier than that). And it was not so much what they said as how they lived that had the biggest impact on my life. My mother was a selfless woman and my father a very charitable man. He always gave and taught us the value of giving. I remember vividly my father's funeral in Montreal because a thousand people attended the funeral and I didn't even know that he knew a thousand people. Many of them kept coming up to me telling me how my father had made such a difference in their life."

But what Harvey remembers most of all was a man who came up to him and told him something he did not know about his father: "When I was growing up there was a great deal of Jewish immigration to Canada, people coming from Eastern Europe and Germany. There was an organization called the Hebrew Free Loan Association which made interest-free loans to these new immigrants. A man came up to me at the funeral and told me that in the early days of the association my father had cosigned every single loan." And yet he had never mentioned it to Harvey, even once in his life. Harvey learned from his mother and father that being charitable created good not only in the lives of others but in the lives of those who give.

Of course we are part of this chain of giving whether we have children or not. Antony was part of it through his teaching. Harvey's father was part of it through his charitable works that inspired other charitable works. And each of us either causes the fire of love and life to burn more brightly because we are here or we cause it to burn less brightly. What I learned in these interviews is that when we give more than we take, we feel connected to the larger story that gives our life purpose. I learned that we can lose ourselves in this larger story.

As I listened to these many voices of people near the end of their lives, I could not help but realize that we are all a part of a much larger chain of life than we realize. We enter the world believing that we are alone and that our one life matters more than any other life. We find our sense of self in the world, but then we come to a time when we recognize that we are part of a much larger conversation. Many of those I interviewed talked to me about realizing that they were a very small part of a much larger landscape. We find happiness ultimately by joining that larger story, focusing less on ourselves and our small concerns and joining something wider and grander. Many of the spiritual traditions focus on this paradox: that it is only by surrendering the ego, the focus on self, that we find true happiness.

Although my focus in the interviews was on finding happiness and purpose at any age, I believe these people also taught me a great deal about vital aging. One of the most profound things I learned about getting older is that the happiest people we interviewed were the least focused on themselves. There are few things more disheartening than an older person who is focused on self and the small concerns of one human life. What I found is that the happiest people had lived full lives, had discovered what was important to them, and were now focused on what they would leave behind.

Over several months, as I listened to the perspectives of people over 60, I became increasingly aware that we live in a borrowed world. Each generation "borrows" the world from the one that came before it and holds it in trust for those yet to arrive. Each generation is a steward of this great gift while it is ours. What I noticed among these people was the recognition that happiness comes both from giving and a deep sense of responsibility to the future.

Chief Ralph, in his sixties, was the elected leader of an aboriginal group on Vancouver Island in western Canada. Since he was an elected chief, rather than a hereditary chief, he had been chosen not because of his ancestry but had been selected by his people because of his qualities as a person. He told me a beautiful story about an experience he had as a teenaged boy.

"We lived on the Pacific Ocean, and each year there was a large salmon run. We all looked forward to going out on the boat and catching fish, which we needed for food during the winter. One year, when my brothers and I were all teenagers, we went out on the boat with my father early in the morning. The fish were so plentiful that in only a few short hours the boat was loaded with salmon, and we had to come back. We three brothers were so excited and hurried to get the fish off the boat so we could go out and catch more."

Chief Ralph continued: "When we told our father that we were ready to go out again, he said, 'no, we are finished.' We asked him why. We knew there were many more fish to catch. But my father said, 'no, we have enough already. We must leave some for others.' We spent the next two days helping other tribe members mend their nets so they too could have enough. That is what I remember."

To me this is a beautiful story at many different levels. The young teenaged boys represent so much of what we believe to be true early in our lives. We set out to catch as many fish as we can catch. We believe that happiness will be found in the number of experiences we have or possessions we gain. Later, often too late, we discover that love, service, and connection to larger purpose are the true food of the human soul. Ralph's father knew that he lived in a borrowed world. It was important to take enough to eat, but it was also important to take no more than was needed. The fish did not belong to his family or even to his community. The fish were borrowed from generations past and held in trust for many generations yet to come. His father, I suspected, knew that the most important lesson he had to give his teenage sons was not a lesson in fishing technique but the lesson that giving to others was the greatest pleasure a human being can have.

A week after Chief Ralph told me that story, I read that over 80% of the world's fisheries are near collapse. We have fished the waters of our world with little regard for those yet to come. Another native elder, White Standing Buffalo, whose life had been saved from the freezing lake, put this in perspective for me. He told me: "In our tradition we believe in a spiral of life. Humans are at the top of the spiral, but this does not make us the most important, only the most vulnerable. We are dependent on all other living things, not more important than them." But it is not too late for us to learn the lessons of the elders.

It seems to me that just as individual human beings find increased happiness when they see their life in service of a greater good, so an entire generation of humans (or a society) must live by this fifth secret. When a generation or society becomes focused on the accumulation of more things and comfort rather than some greater sense of purpose, a society, like a person, loses its vitality. Like an individual human being, the more a society focuses on the needs of the "small self," which come in the form of luxuries, material possessions, and personal happiness, the more that society is likely to deteriorate. However, when we focus on our core purpose as a collective, which is to hand off a better world to the next generation, we find a deep sense of purpose.

When I was in Tanzania spending time with tribal elders in several communities, I often asked the elders if they were worried about the future. Their common response was "of course we are worried about the future." In talking to the elders we interviewed for this book, I discovered that they, too, are deeply worried about the future. Many of them expressed deep concern about the increasing tension between religions, the wholesale destruction of the planet's environment, and our seeming unwillingness to sacrifice for the future. But I also discovered that their greatest source of happiness had often come from feeling in some small way they had contributed to making things better.

learn to cry for the world, not for yourself

Susan, 68, told me that "as I have aged I find I no longer cry for myself but I cry for the world. Part of getting older is that you realize you will not be here forever but that the story goes on beyond you." When she said these words, I realized that the happiest people we interviewed had learned to cry for the world and that those who were most unhappy were still crying for themselves. And we can learn this lesson when we are young or in mid-life; our greatest happiness will come from what we give away.

It is a beautiful image. From the 200 people, I discovered that as we age some of us cry for ourselves (for our own disappointments and regrets), while some of us learn to cry for the world. When we learn to cry for the world and not ourselves we lose ourselves in that larger story.

"What matters is how we treat each other," Susan told me, "and how we interact with the environment. We must think about our impact on the future."

Perhaps happiness cannot really be pursued. Perhaps it is a by-product of something more profound. Juana, 64, said "if you are unhappy, get busy doing something for someone else. If you concentrate on yourself you will be unhappy, but if you focus on helping others you will find happiness. Happiness comes from serving and loving."

When my oldest daughter Lena was in high school, she announced that her goal in life was to "become famous." Intrigued, I asked what she wished to become famous for? "It doesn't matter," she said "I just want people to know my name." Apparently she is not alone; a recent survey showed that as many as one-third of high school students had the goal of having fame. In a world addicted to reality shows and the buzz of 15 minutes of fame (often for nothing of great significance), being known had somehow replaced finding significance. At the time, I told her that fame without contribution would have little meaning, but contribution without fame would be its own reward. She gave me the look most teenagers give on hearing such advice.

These interviews convinced me more than ever of the value of those words I shared with her. The happiest people I interviewed knew their life had mattered, that they had been of service. The most miserable people had focused on themselves and finding happiness, getting love, accumulating things, status and "fame."

Talking to older people gave me a new perspective on an old truth: We live in a borrowed world. The happiest people were those who knew they had left things better than they had found them in some small way, whether in the form of children who were contributing, the small advancement of a cause, or leaving their impact on a small group of people.

But does each one of us really have the capability to change the world? One of the things we are learning from the world of physics is how things are far more interconnected than we ever imagined. Atomic particles separated by physical space interact with one another and influence movement. The same is true of the world of human affairs. Each one of us changes the "movement" of the world by the way we interact with it. Taken together these subtle changes shape the future. Robert Kennedy once wrote: "Few will have the greatness to bend history; but each of us can work to change a small portion of events, and in the total of all those acts will be written the history of a generation . . . It is from numberless diverse acts of courage and belief that human history is thus shaped. Each time a man stands up for an ideal, or acts to improve the lot of others, or strikes out against injustice, he sends forth a tiny ripple of hope, and crossing each other from a million different centers of energy and daring, those ripples build a current which can sweep down the mightiest walls of oppression and resistance."

I recall vividly the first time I really saw the Milky Way. Having grown up in a large urban area, I rarely saw more than a few stars at night. But in college, I found myself doing a work tour on the islands of Bermuda. At the time, there were few electric lights on the outer islands. One night, around midnight, we walked to the top of a hill and lay down on the grass facing the dark night sky. With the sound of tree frogs dancing in my ears, I saw the Milky Way for the first time. There above me was a part of the sky so dense with stars that it looked like the creator had thrown milk across the sky. The sight was even more inspiring because I remembered learning that the Milky Way is not actually "out there," because our solar system (the Sun and all the planets) is in the middle of the galaxy known as the Milky Way. I was looking up and seeing something that was all around me.

As I was admiring the sky, I remembered something I had learned in an astronomy class: that many of the stars we see at night may no longer exist. They are so far away from our earth that it takes millions of years for their light to reach us. I was seeing the light of some stars that were already extinguished.

At 19, I remember thinking that some people's lives were like that, shining a light in the world long after they were gone. I said a prayer that I would live that kind of life.

The fifth secret is to *give more than we take*. When we give more than we take we connect ourselves to a story bigger than ourselves. And in the act of doing so, happiness finds us.

Here are some questions to think about each week to help you live this secret:

- Did I make the world a better place this week in some small way?

- Did I remind myself this week that I am making a difference even if I don't see it?

- Was I kind, generous, and giving this week? How do I want to be more that way tomorrow/next week?

- Was I focused on the needs of the "small self" this week (the pursuit of things, status, or power) rather than the "larger self" (which is my contribution to making the world around me a better place)?

- How do I want to live this secret more deeply next week?

when you know you have to go (putting the secrets into practice)

The problem with common sense is that it is not common
—Mark Twain

Wisdom is knowing what to do next; virtue is doing it.
—David Starr Jordan

I reached a turning point in the interviewing process while listening to 71-year-old Ron, the man who followed his own heart to become a chiropractor, drowning out the voices of others in the process. As did so many of the people I interviewed, he had a calm, centered presence that mirrored the words he shared with me about his life. He helped me see that knowing the secrets is not enough.

Ron attributed his happiness to following his heart. At several key times in his life, his heart had told him that he needed to make a change, and each time he heeded its call. In each case, in order to "follow his heart" something had been required of him: sometimes courage, often a willingness to ignore other voices, and most of all the choice to act on what he knew to be true. I asked him: "How did you know when you were following your heart?"

"I guess I just knew. It's hard to explain, but it is as though I could hear this voice telling me what to do. Maybe it is that

way for most people in that we know what we want to do. But
we have to have the discipline to listen, and then we have to
have the courage to follow. What I have found is that when you
know, you have to go, it is simply not enough to know."

The moment he spoke, I knew he had said something
simple and incredibly important. For many people the greatest block is not the knowing but the going. Maybe many of us
know the secrets to happiness and purpose, but we simply don't
live them. Knowing is only the first step.

knowing is not the problem

Think of all the things we know and fail to act on. We know
smoking kills us, that lack of exercise, poor eating habits and
stress can kill us, too. We know that relationships are important
and often fragile, but we often neglect them anyway. We know
that money will not buy happiness, and that life is short, and that
negative, self-defeating thoughts can destroy our happiness. We
know so many things, but knowing is not enough.

Consider for a moment, the research findings about patients with coronary artery disease (blocked arteries). After having procedures to save their lives, or even having near-death experiences, these patients are asked to make a rather stark choice:
Change or die. Faced with the almost certain knowledge that
blocked arteries will kill them if they don't change their lifestyle,
almost all of them, we think, would change. Change or die is a
pretty straightforward choice. But the research shows that over
70% fail to make changes. This tells me that for many of us it is
at least as important to know how to live the secrets as it is to
know the secrets.

I am certain that the five secrets found in this book—*being
true to your self, leaving no regrets, becoming love, living the mo-*

ment, and giving more than you take—are the essential building blocks of a happy, purposeful life. I am also fairly certain that many of you knew some or most of these secrets *before* you read this book. Your heart has been telling you this all of your life. But how do we put these secrets into practice in our lives? How do *we go*, now that *we know*? I believe these interviews provide the answer to this question as well.

natural learning: how we make changes in our lives

In this chapter, we explore ways we can make changes in our lives and then apply this knowledge specifically to living the five secrets. To understand how we implement change in our lives, consider the natural learning process by which human beings develop. By the natural learning process, I mean the process by which we learn most of the skills we need for daily living, such as language and motor skills.

Language acquisition serves as a great example of natural learning. During my many years of school, I have taken courses and studied at least six languages (Latin, Greek, Hebrew, French, Spanish, and Italian). In spite of all those courses, I can neither write nor speak more than one full sentence in any language except English. However, by the time I was only a few years old I had mastered English, even though many linguists consider it a difficult language to learn. Why can a young child master her native tongue but later in life take second-language courses without, perhaps, ever mastering one?

Part of the answer lies in the fact that we humans learn naturally by watching, listening, and experimenting. Most of our early language acquisition does not come through formal attempts to teach us language. Rather, we watch our mothers and fathers wander around calling things by name. We listen to them talk and listen to how sentences are woven together. With only a small amount of correction, we learn vocabulary and then how to use those words to build sentences. We learn naturally by watching, imitating, and by experimenting.

The same can be said of walking. How did you learn to walk? I can still remember the day my oldest daughter Lena took her first steps on her own. She had been able to stand for some time; then, one day in the bathroom, my wife was standing about five feet away from her and said "come here." With a lurching gait she walked the five feet to our cheers and her giggles. Without one formal lesson on walking she had learned to walk. But how? Once again, the answer is simple: natural learning. She watched and observed, then she experimented until she was walking. Another way to describe this natural-learning process is to say it has two simple steps: *awareness and experimentation.* We pay attention, and we try things. In the process of doing these two things, we constantly self-correct until we achieve mastery.

Let's apply this simple idea of natural learning to making complicated changes in our adult lives. If awareness is the first step of the natural learning process, then it can be said that *we move toward what we hold in our awareness.* This is a simple idea with profound consequences for making change in our lives. *We become what we pay attention to. The more we hold something in our awareness, the more likely we are to move toward that thing.*

what we pay attention to grows

A number of years ago we conducted a research study involving several hundred people who were trying to make simple but important changes in their lives (such as losing weight, exercising more regularly, eating in a healthier way, speaking up more, having more balance, and so on). These hundreds of people were brought together, and then the group was split in half. Each group was led through a process to identify the changes they wanted to make in their lives (*the knowing*).

Next the two groups were given two very different methods to implement change (*the going*). One group set very specific goals for themselves, such as to run three times a week, to eat only healthy foods for ten weeks, and so forth. They were asked to write these goals down and review them once each week for the next twelve weeks.

The second group was given a very different method to implement change. They were given cards and asked to write down a few words or phrases that would remind them of the change they wanted to make in their life (eat healthy, be more active, speak up for yourself, take time for self). They were then asked to carry the card with them wherever they went for the next 12 weeks. Ten to twenty times per day they were to take the card out, look at it, and to be aware of the choices they were making. Carry the card, look at it many times, and never go anywhere without the card. They were also told not to beat themselves up, not to engage in negative self-talk, but to simply be aware of these things as they went through their day.

Twelve weeks later, both groups had made progress, but one group achieved a great deal more change (as much as three times more)—and that was the group who carried the cards. *Through the simple act of paying attention, change occurred.*

It is worthwhile to dissect this experiment and to understand why the simple act of holding something in your awareness produces significant change. Remember, the "natural" way we learn is by paying attention and experimenting. This is how we learned the most complex tasks of our early life: walking and our native language. The process of holding something in our awareness mirrors that natural process. By holding something in front of us and by experimenting, we create change.

But why was the simple act of carrying a card around superior to goal setting? This is an important question. I believe the answer is simple. Although goal setting activates our awareness, it may negatively affect experimentation. For example, the person who sets a goal to run three times per week will hold that idea in his awareness and may even achieve it. However, what happens if during the first week he injures himself and can't run the next week? What happens if it turns out that he doesn't enjoy running very much? The most likely outcome is that he feels a sense of failure and so aborts attempts to change. What's more, he will likely miss many other opportunities to become more active that are available during the day.

Contrast this person with the one who simply carries a card with the words "be more active and physically fit." Because she looks at that card 10–20 times each day, she may make numerous decisions that will affect her health. She may read the card and then take the stairs instead of the elevator, or take a walk during lunch rather than sit at her desk. When she reads the card, she may call a friend right then to set up a game of tennis. Awareness breeds experimentation. Of course goal setting and awareness can be combined for even greater effect, but if I had to suggest only one method to create change in your life, I would begin with the card you carry all day long.

A few examples of this technique in action are useful. About eight years ago I came to a very difficult realization. At the age of 41, I realized that I had a great career, a great family life, and hundreds of acquaintances. What I also realized was that I had no true friends. So much of my energy had been put into work that I had fenced friendship out of my adult life. It was quite frightening to realize that after 40 years I had no enduring friendships. I knew I had to do something about it—but what to do?

Following my own advice, I wrote down the word "friends" on a card and began carrying it around with me. Ten to twenty times each day I took the card out and looked at it. To be honest, the first few weeks were kind of depressing, because many times each day I would look at that card and become deeply aware of how much I had neglected this part of my life. I worked hard not to beat myself up but to simply become aware—*to pay attention*—to how important friendship was for me.

After about two weeks of carrying the card around, I decided that if I was going to make some friends the first step was to have some "prospects"—kind of like a list of girls to invite to the high school prom. So I listed all the acquaintances I had who I believed could become friends. I came up with a list of six people. Over the next few months, I began calling these people and setting up lunches, coffee meetings, and occasionally a social get-together. I did not tell them "I am looking for friends and you are on the list." I just started paying attention and experimenting in the moment.

One experience I had during this time demonstrates the simple power of the card. I was then board president of a nonprofit organization. One night after a long meeting, having already calculated how many hours of sleep I wanted, I eagerly prepared to go home. Another member of the board, Bryan, asked me if I wanted to go out and get a bite to eat with him after the meeting. I was about to say no when I literally felt the card in my pocket. Bryan was not on the list, but he seemed like a person whom I would enjoy getting to know. The card turned my no into a yes. Some time later, he became a friend.

I carried the card around with me for almost 18 months, by which time six people had become friends, three of whom were on my original list and three who were not. Now, years later, whenever I find myself neglecting this important aspect of my life, my mind easily conjures the image of that card and gently moves me back toward what matters.

Having taught this technique for many years now, I have heard numerous stories of the power of the "card" to produce change in people's lives. One woman told me that the biggest thing she wanted to work on in her life was her relationship with her teenaged stepson. "We are always at each other," she said, "and I think the key is that I react to him with negativity." So she wrote down on a card these simple words "don't react to Nathan." Within two months, she reported that her relationship with him had changed dramatically for the better. Every time she was about to react negatively, she remembered the card she was carrying and adjusted her approach. The payoff was immense in terms of her personal happiness.

Another person decided to work on being kinder to each person he encountered, including those he loved the most. He began carrying a card around with him wherever he went. After several weeks, the people in his life both at work and at home began commenting about the significant change they had seen in him and wondered what was going on. He simply smiled and kept carrying the card. Within a few short months, he wrote me a letter to tell me that his relationship with his wife and his relationships at work had been radically improved by that small card.

Now you may be tempted to simply take out a card and write down the five secrets and carry the card with you for the next several months. Although this is not a bad idea, it is not recommended. Human beings are not very good parallel processors. If we are working on too many things at once, we often become paralyzed and unable to act. It is as if, when we act on too many things at once, we wind up acting on nothing.

Instead, think back over this book's five secrets. Which one secret seems most in need of your attention right now? Work on this one secret and, if possible, choose a specific focus within that secret. Here's an example: Perhaps you believe that the most important secret for you right now is to *become love*. In particular, you feel that making more time for family is critical for you. You might write on the card *become love and make time for family*. Perhaps the most important secret for you right now is to *leave no regrets (risk more)*. As part of that secret, taking more risks in meeting new people might become your focus. So you might carry a card around with the words: *leave no regrets and meet new people*.

Make a commitment to carry that card around for the next few months. Commit to looking at it ten to twenty times each day. But don't just look at the card; become aware of the choices that you are making *moment to moment*. Make a commitment to carrying the card until you can honestly say that you have made significant progress toward your intention. As I mentioned earlier, I carried my friendship reminder card for 18 months. I did not stop carrying it until I could honestly say that I had made real gains in making friendship a priority (not to mention having some friends). Many times when we attempt to make changes in our lives, we try to make changes for a short period of time but quit before the change is significant or before the new habits become strong enough to be sustainable.

This simple technique of writing your intention down on a card and carrying it with you has applications in many realms of life For example, a couple I know intended to begin a business together. They had separate careers, but each person wrote down on a card the intention to create a certain kind of business together. Several years later, it became reality. Remember, the key principle is this: What we hold in our awareness we move toward naturally.

change begins with the first question

Another technique for "going when we know" I learned from my friend Marshall Goldsmith, author of *What Got You Here Won't Get You There,* who is one of the world's leading personal development coaches. He told me that he has a list of 18 questions that he asks himself every day. These questions cause him to reflect on whether his life was "on target" that particular day. The questions are very specific, such as: Did you get angry today? Did you act in a loving way toward your wife? Once each day he checks in with himself and tries to honestly answer these questions.

Like the act of carrying a card, having a list of questions to ask yourself each day or week is a great way of using the natural-learning process: *pay attention and experiment.* By asking these questions at least once each week, or perhaps daily, we hold these things in constant awareness. As we reflect, we begin to think about ways to experiment and shift our life toward a more ideal state.

One of the most important things the interviews taught me is the importance of self-correction and reflection in finding happiness and purpose. The people we interviewed were not born wiser than the rest of us. In fact, many of them talked to me about how much they had learned and grown over the years through the simple process of regular reflection, followed by corrective action. Their lives were the result of years of small adjustments that cumulatively created the happiness that others saw in them.

Many of us will be able to live more fully simply by reflecting more. One way of doing this is to define a set of questions that focus on the five secrets and to set aside a small amount of time each week to reflect on your life. Another way is to create your own set of personal questions. At the end of this chapter, I list 24 questions you might ask yourself each week during a time of reflection. Here's an example (under the heading of the first secret, *be true to yourself*): Did this feel like my kind of day or week? If so, how did it feel like my kind of week? If not, what felt out of alignment with my truest self? So, the steps of the natural-learning process—*awareness and experimentation*—are respected in this method. But there is one more element of natural learning that helps us go where we know we want to go.

Earlier we explored the idea that some of the most basic life skills, such as walking and language development, were learned through the natural-learning process. In this process we learn by paying attention and by experimenting. The card and the questions are two approaches to effecting this process, especially if, each time you look at the card or ask your questions, you take the additional step of asking what small changes you can do right now to act on this awareness. Still, there is one element of the natural-learning process that I have not yet covered.

we change best when we change together

When we learned to walk and talk, we did not do it alone. Most of us had a coach every step of the way. Our parents, siblings, and relatives were there to hold us accountable. When we said "da da," they said "you mean daddy." They also encouraged us. When we stood up for the first time and fell back down, they likely did not say "what a clumsy fool you are!" More likely they said something like "good girl, try again. Maybe try holding the table first." I wonder if people would ever learn to walk and talk without the coaching and simple encouragement of others. Yet, often as adults we try to make changes in our lives without any accountability to or encouragement from others.

When Marshall told me about the daily questions, he also mentioned that each day a friend called him and asked him the 18 questions. Every day they would check in with each other both to hold each other accountable and to encourage each other. Why not team up with someone else who is reading this book—someone who is interested in putting the secrets into practice. Check in with each other, encourage each other, and offer ideas for self-correction. We change best when we change together.

Here's another simple technique to act on what you know. Take 30 to 60 minutes each week to reflect on your life. There is a saying in the Christian monastic tradition, "sit in your cell, and your cell will teach you everything." When we take time to reflect, we often know what we need to do. The answers are within us. The discipline to listen is critical. We have only one life, at least here, and the time goes by very fast. Time for reflection, for listening, is the way we keep our life from drifting away from our intentions. Earlier I used the analogy of archery, noting that the word for "sin" in ancient Greek means to "miss the mark." When we build in weekly or daily reflection to determine whether we are "hitting the mark," we allow for the natural, small self-corrections that ultimately create a good life.

One woman I interviewed reminded me that "you can't be listening to your soul while you are watching *The Simpsons*." We live in a time when reflection is often fenced out of our lives as we fill our days with tasks and our nights with noise. Even when we arrive at a hotel room alone, we often turn on the TV. Yet choosing to be quiet and to listen to those still small voices inside us are important keys to life well-lived. Make a commitment to a weekly time of reflection. Ask if your life is on target and how you want to change in the coming week. Imagine, over time, the massive power of small self-corrections made over many years. Like compounded interest on a savings account, small changes in our lives add up to significant results. However, failing to take time to reflect is like compounding interest on your credit card. Small balances over time may become a debt that can never be repaid.

what are the rituals of your life?

The interview conversations also reminded me of the power of rituals. As I listened to these wise people, I realized that many of them had used such rituals to help them live the secrets more deeply. We tend to associate ritual with formal religion, but a ritual can be any practice or pattern of behavior regularly performed in a set manner. For some people, a visit to a particular coffee shop can serve as an important morning ritual. Some rituals are mere routine, but others have the power, over time, to shape our experience of living.

Sixty-two-year-old Joel told me about two rituals that have shaped his life. When he wakes up in the morning, the first thing he does is have a time of meditation. "I thank God for another day and take a few minutes to remind myself what a gift it is to be alive, to be a conscious being in the middle of the Milky Way. In that time of meditation I ask that I might act today like this is a great gift and that I would not waste the day ahead." He went on to tell me that he ends each day with a similar meditation. "At the end of the day, I take a few minutes of meditation and review the day, taking note of all the things which I am grateful for from that day, however small they may be. And before I go to sleep, I pray that I might have one more day to enjoy being alive."

Lea is 58 and an incredibly busy person. Each morning before she leaves her home she, too, makes time for meditation. "Each morning I take time for being quiet. Often I read something that will get me in the right frame of mind for the day. And each day I say a prayer asking that I will notice those in my path for whom a kind word, a smile, a thank you might be life changing, and I pray that I will not be so busy during my day to miss that."

Then there was Jim, who said that for many years he took walks that were "ranting" walks. He would walk and contemplate all the things that angered him about the world. One day he decided to begin taking "gratitude" walks. "Now while I walk I recount all the things I am grateful for in my life and don't allow myself to think of negative things at all. I have found this simple practice to be a great gift."

Many years ago, I met a middle-aged nurse who worked in a hospital cancer unit. Each day she spent hours in the presence of suffering. She told me that she had a theme song she played on her way to work. It was a particular song that reminded her each day of what a gift it was to be alive, a song that lifted her spirit. She told me, "by the time I am at work, I am ready for the day!"

As I listened to these and many other stories like them, I began to realize the power that rituals have to change us. It was not hard to imagine the effect that years of starting and ending each day with a time of meditation, thanking the universe for another day and ending the day in gratitude, might have on how a person experiences life. I could imagine how that morning ritual reminded Lea every day that what mattered was to give and that she had the power to give from the moment she left the house until her return. I could see that nurse singing her heart away every morning because that one song somehow put her in just the right place to start her day. Rituals are so important that we must be very careful what rituals we allow or choose to become routine. Jim took those "rant" walks for many years before he turned them into "gratitude" walks.

A good first step to determining your rituals is to become aware of the rituals that already exist in your life. How do you begin your day? What is the mood you set? How do you end your day? What are the last thoughts that you take with you into your dreams? What rituals lift your spirit, and what ones may be diminishing it? Over time, as we become more conscious of the rituals that shape us, we become more able to shape them. I begin my day by reading my personal vision statement, which begins with these three words: I am content. By reading this statement each morning I send a prayer to my self-conscious about my life intention before the day takes on a life of its own.

Thoughts and words are the powerful beginning of a chain that defines how we live. Years ago I read a saying that I thought of many times as I listened to people tell me about their lives: "Be careful of your thoughts, because your thoughts become your words. Be careful with your words, because your words become your actions. Be careful of your actions, because your actions become your habits. Be careful of your habits, because your habits become your character. And your character becomes your destiny."

There are many other techniques for turning wisdom into action, but I believe that the methods discussed here form the foundation of acting on what we know. Knowledge of what makes a life happy and purposeful means little if this knowledge is not translated into action. Knowing and going. We must do both.

Joel, the 62-year-old futurist, told me that "action without vision is simply using up your time, but vision without action is only a daydream." The secrets are the vision, the methods in this chapter a path to action. Knowing the secrets will not change your life, living them will.

Weekly/Daily Reflection Questions on the Five Secrets

Secret	Question for Reflection
	• Did this week or day feel like my kind of week/ day? What would make tomorrow or next week feel more true to myself?
Be True to Your Self (Reflect More)	• Was I the kind of person I want to be this week? In what way can I be more like the kind of person I want to be tomorrow or next week?
	• Am I following my heart right now? What would it mean for me to really follow my heart right now?
	• How do I want to live this secret more deeply next week?
	• Did I act out of fear today or this week? How do I want to be more courageous tomorrow or next week?
	• Did I act on my convictions this week? How do I want to act on them more deeply this week?
Leave No Regrets (Risk More)	• What step would I take in my life right now if I were acting with courage, not fear?
	• What would the "old man or woman on the porch" say about the decisions I am making in my life right now? Am I planting regrets?
	• How am I responding to the setbacks in my life right now? Am I stepping forward or retreating?
	• How do I want to live this secret more deeply next week?

Become Love (Love More)	• Did I make room for friends, family, and relationships today/this week? • Was I kind and loving today/this week to the people closest to me? How can I be more loving to them tomorrow or this week? • Did I spread love and kindness in the world today/this week in each interaction? Did I act as if each stranger was someone for whom I could make a difference? • Which of my two wolves did I feed today/this week? Did I spend time with people who lift my spirit? Did I act with love toward myself today/this week? Did I engage in negative self-talk/self-hypnosis? Am I planting flowers or weeds in my self-conscious mind? • How do I want to live this secret more deeply next week?
Live the Moment (Enjoy More)	• Did I fully enjoy whatever I was doing this week or day? Was I really "here" or just showing up? • Did I take every pleasure that was available to me today/this week (really smell the flowers), and did I walk through my life or just run? • What am I grateful for about today/this week? Did I find myself saying "I would be happy if"? • Did I live in the present today/this week, or did I let tomorrow or yesterday steal the day's happiness? • Did I wake up this morning with thanks for another day? • How do I want to live this secret more deeply next week?

continued

Give More Than You Take (Return More)	• Did I make the world a better place this week in some small way?
	• Did I remind myself this week that I am making a difference even when I don't see it?
	• Was I kind, generous, and giving this week? How can I be more that way tomorrow/next week?
	• How do I want to live this secret more deeply next week?
Area of Focus	*For the next week, what I want to pay more attention to is . . . (choose only one thing)*

chapter nine

preparing to die well: happy people are not afraid to die

Even death is not to be feared by those who live wisely.
—Buddha

My father-in-law is in his early sixties and in excellent health. While having dinner at our home last year he announced, out of the blue, that he had been thinking about his death. He had decided that he did not want any crying at his funeral (at which point, of course, my wife began crying). He went on to say that it was very important to him that we all knew that he was not afraid of death.

"When I was younger," he told us, "I remember being afraid of death, but now that I am closer to it I have no fear of it." What ensued was one of the most moving experiences of my life—an emotional and touching conversation about my father-in-law's life. Many tears were shed, and a great deal of loving words exchanged. In the end, he had given his family a great gift by being willing to talk about what we all know: that one day we will die.

This conversation occurred about two months before we began what I came to call "the wise elder project." So, when we began the interviews I added a question I had not anticipated asking: "Now that you are older, tell me how your view of your mortality has changed. How do you feel about death, not the abstract idea of dying, but your own death?" As a mid-life person approaching 50, I wanted to know how these people who had lived a wise and purposeful life felt about their mortality.

Talking to 200 over the age of 60 about death is very different than talking to 30-year-olds or even mid-lifers about dying. Many of these people had experienced the loss of those closest to them (wives, husbands, partners, parents, and dear friends), and many of them had had near-death experiences. They told me that they contemplated their mortality on a more regular basis as they got closer to dying, or as 86-year-old Antony told me, "now that I am beyond my best-used-before date." For these people, death was not some distant possibility but a real part of their daily mental landscape.

Yet, what I learned in talking to these people was inspiring, profound, and in the end deeply comforting.

The most beautiful gift I can share with you as a reader is to tell you that, of these 230 people, fewer than you could count on one hand expressed any fear about dying. Almost all of them had integrated the awareness of death into life. What I discovered is that when we live wisely, we do not fear death. If we live the five secrets found in this book, we will not be afraid to die. It is only when we have *not* lived wisely, when we have not lived by the secrets, do we have anything to fear.

One of my good friends, David Kuhl, is a gifted physician who has spent a great deal of time with dying patients (and based on his research with the dying wrote a beautiful book titled *What Dying People Want*). When I told him what I had discovered in these interviews, he told me that in his work with dying persons he had discovered that "happy people are not afraid to die." It seems a bit ironic of course, because you would think that those who love life would be most afraid to die, but he had found among younger people who were dying the same thing that I discovered among the old. We die as we live. If we have lived our life with wisdom, we can accept death as part of life. "I am not nervous about dying," 59-year-old Bob told me. "When I go, I will have a smile on my face; I feel good about my life, my legacy, and how I have lived my life. I remember my dad telling me that he wished he had lived his life differently, and I pledged that I would not do that. The most important thing is to do what you came here to do, and I have done that."

Again and again, people told me that when we have lived wisely, we will not fear death. In fact, when I asked people to tell me what the greatest fear is at the end of life, it was not death that people spoke of, but of not having lived.

Tom, 64, is the Metis native whose spiritual name is White Standing Buffalo. For almost 20 years he had been leading spiritual ceremonies within his community. He told me that in his tradition death is not something to be feared but a natural part of the process of living. "What we fear at the end of our life is the great incompleteness; that we did not do what we were born to do. Death is part of life, but to embrace death, we must know we have lived."

Seventy-one-year-old Elsa expressed similar sentiments. "The biggest fear at the end of life is that you did not do everything you could have done, that you have never really lived. If we want to prepare to die, we must choose to live fully so that we leave no regrets," she told me. It was a theme that I heard many times.

Many of these people had had near-death experiences. Uniformly, they told me that the most interesting element of these experiences was the awareness that it was not unpleasant—that when the moment comes for us to die it does not arrive with fear and sorrow. Dick, in his seventies, told me about a near-death experience: "When I was in my fifties, I had a heart procedure, and during the test my heart stopped for a prolonged time. I can still remember feeling my self rising out of my body and looking down on the physician and nurses trying to revive me. I could hear them saying 'stay with us, come on, stay with us.' I did not see a white light, nor did I meet Jesus, but I realized it was not unpleasant. There was a great calm. Since then I have not been afraid of death at all."

One of the most beautiful stories was told to me by Elsa. "My mother was not a religious woman. When I was young, I had a prized doll that was destroyed, and I asked my mother if the doll was now in heaven. She told me right out that there is no heaven when you are dead; that when you die you are simply dead!" Later in her life, Elsa would develop a deep personal faith, and God became an important part of her life. Her mother, however, never became a religious person.

"When my mother was dying I went to stay with her. One day it was a very cloudy, dark day, and the blinds were open in her bedroom. Suddenly the sky brightened and light shined in the room. My mother had this look of awe and peace on her face. When I asked if she wanted me to close the shades she insisted that I not close out the light. So I asked her what she saw and she told me: 'It is so beautiful, but I cannot explain it to you. When your time comes you will see it.' The next day she died." Elsa has carried that moment in her mind as she has aged, believing that when her moment comes she will see what her mother saw that day.

Many of these people talked to me about being able to see across now to the other side. As different as their belief systems were, they seemed to have found a way to integrate death into their lives. As they looked ahead, there was a common sense of peace that I sensed among them. Some of them saw a foreshadow of heaven, others a more subtle awareness that they would some-how connect to the larger landscape from which they had come. Listening to them made me think of the words of Derek Walcott, the Nobel-Prize-winning poet from St. Lucia, who wrote in his book *The Prodigal* about how as he gets closer to death he can see "dolphins dancing on the bow and the outline of the silhou-ette of home." Walcott wrote about how, when he was younger, he would never have imagined this feeling of peace as he grew nearer to the end of his life. Like Elsa's mother looking out the window and like my father-in-law, who said he had feared death as a younger man but had now found peace with it, Walcott had found a quiet in him that he had not anticipated.

Some of these people even told me that preparing to die well is one of the most important things a human being must do as they age. Jack, 67, told me this: "I am at the age now that my Dad died. I expect to live a while longer, but I have been thinking a good deal more about dying lately. I am not sure what happens to us when we die, but I am comfortable. I guess that if there is justice, and I think there is, that I will get fair treatment. Many of my friends have died, so I have had the privilege of watching peo-ple die. A good friend of mine had ALS [Lou Gehrig's disease], and he decided he wanted his friends to be around him while he was dying. He made it comfortable for people, and I did his eulogy. I was there a few days before he died, and he could barely speak. I had to put my ear by his mouth to hear him, but he was still spirited and kept his sense of humor. I remember thinking that I wanted to die that way as well."

When I asked him what it meant to him to "die well," he told me: "To die well is not to complain, to continue to have a good spirit, and to let those who are still living know that it is ok, it is a part of life. This is the last gift we give. The last direct influence you can have is how you die."

Maybe all our lives we are preparing to die well. Maybe until we learn to live we cannot die with grace, or maybe it is the other way around. Maybe we cannot live until we assimilate the truth of our mortality. Ron, 71, told me that "the last cycle of the 'evening of your life' is about preparing to die, to learn to let go of it. Until you learn to die, you don't know how to live. Until you incorporate your understanding of your assimilation in the end, you don't know how to live your life. It can be to-morrow or 20 years from now. You don't know. But if you learn to embrace it as part of life then you can live." Death gives life its urgency, but also since we will ALL die, until we can accept and embrace this truth, we cannot live with hope.

In the end, these conversations showed me that living wisely is the antidote to the fear of death. They also showed me that as we age, one of the most important tasks is to prepare to die well, to give the final gift of hope to those who are left behind. I also discovered that when we realize that we are part of a much larger story, our death becomes something we can accept with grace.

Listening to people talk about their own death in calm, strong voices led me to realize that perhaps the greatest delusion in life is that we are separate from everything around us. In one way or another, these several hundred people told me that they knew that in death they would be reunited with something more fundamental and that until a human being realizes that we, and our singular ego, are not separate but connected, we will always be in despair. John, the painter in his mid-nineties, told me: "We are only a speck, really, but we are part of something larger, and when we die we reunite with that larger story."

Some of my own most spiritual moments have been when I have experienced this deep connectedness. Years ago I was hiking by a stream in the mountains of Italy near a monastery at which John Milton had written his classic poem, *Paradise Lost*. Walking along the stream and trying to find my place in the world I was overwhelmed with a feeling. As I listened to the stream roll down the mountain, I was aware somehow that I was part of something greater. Kneeling down, alone by a stream that had likely run down this mountain for millennia in one form or another, I submerged my hand in the cold running stream. I realized that I had spent my entire life thinking of my self as separate from the stream, as an entity outside the web of life and creation. I realized that I was one with that stream and with the entire living universe. I felt a deep acceptance not only of my place in the world but also that one day I would again rejoin the stream of life. I, like Walcott wrote in poetic metaphor, could see the "dolphins dancing on the bow."

It may be that, in the end, these conversations taught me as much about how to die well as they did about how to live well. I began to see the intimate connection between living and dying in a way that I had never seen before. As a young minister, I had sat with people who were dying and had noticed that people die very differently. Yet, now I began to see that dying and living were not disconnected. We die as we have lived. When we live wisely we will not fear death; those who feel they have really lived often die peaceful deaths. It is the fear of not having truly lived that makes us afraid to die. Yet, I also came to see that if we are truly wise, we will live always in the shadow of death. Recognizing its presence reminds us that now is the time to live. Maybe Ron was right when he told me that "unless we integrate the knowledge of our death into our life, we are not truly prepared to live fully." Unless we come to peace with death, not as some foreign invader but as a part of what it means to be human, only then can we find peace.

chapter ten

a final lesson: it's never too late to live the secrets

The last gift I received from the interviews was a lesson about timing.

We asked thousands of people to identify one person whom they had known and who had lived long and had found happiness. Going into these interviews, we wondered if the people identified had been wise all their lives. Had they been born with the right genes or raised by the right parents, or were these people just like the rest of us?

The interviewing process does not necessarily let us know when a particular person began to live a certain way. My conclusion is that some of them had been living the secrets since they were quite young, whereas others did not embrace them until quite late in life. Each person I interviewed had learned a great deal through the process of living and had slowly become the person who now sat in front of me. A number of these people had experienced significant turning points, often relatively late in life, when they discovered what really matters. So, the most important thing is not *when* we find the secrets but *that we do* find the secrets. No matter what age we are, or what mistakes we have made, when we embrace and live the five secrets our lives begin to change.

One of the most beautiful qualities of these people was a deep sense of grace. Many of them said that they had been too hard on other people when they were younger, but many of them also said that they had been too hard on themselves. One of the themes I have not discussed yet is the idea of living one's life rather than judging one's life. *Living* our life means that we take our life day to day and moment to moment, always trying to deepen our understanding of what it means to be human. Life will never be perfect, and we will always be in a state of moving toward completeness. Don, 84, put it this way: "You have lived the life you have lived. When we accept the life we have lived, then we can begin to be whole." He echoed an often-heard theme: When we judge our life we diminish ourselves. The more we can eliminate all need to compare, compete, grade, and judge our lives, the closer we get to wisdom.

As you contemplate the five secrets, try to resist the temptation to "judge" your life. Instead, ask: How can I embrace and live the five secrets more deeply? The judging mind paralyzes us either by giving us a false sense of perfection or by giving us a deep sense of inadequacy. We have lived the life we have lived, and now we have the opportunity to grow.

Many years ago, I gave a talk to a group of middle-aged men on the topic of love. In the talk, I focused on how we often fail to treat those closest to us with kindness and love (and on the studies, mentioned earlier, that show that in the average home we give 14 negative/critical messages to other family members for every one positive/appreciative comment). After the talk, a number of people came up to speak with me, and there was one "tough-looking" gentleman who waited until everyone else had finished. He said: "That was a great talk. As I was listening to you today I realized that the way I have been with my family and with other people for most of my life has been destructive. They needed my love, and they have received judgment; they needed my appreciation and got my criticisms; and they needed me to be a positive person, and I have drowned them in negativity. Your talk today has changed my life. I have only one regret: I wish I'd heard you 30 years ago, because I have wasted my life." Tears ran down his weathered cheeks.

His words stung me to the core. He had suddenly come to terms with how he had lived his life and did not like what he saw. I searched for a word of encouragement that I could give him that would encourage this new insight but also help heal his regret. I shared with him a Chinese proverb: "The best time to plant a tree is 20 years ago, but the second best time is today." By planting a new tree today, the legacy of his life would change. It was not too late.

It is never too late to embrace the five secrets found in this book and to change the legacy of many years. Even one year lived wisely can erase many years of regret.

One of my favorite interviews was with John, the 93-year-old painter from Toronto. He had a sparkle of curiosity in his eyes, a warm gentility in his voice, and the hands of an artist, strong and careful. The first 30 years of his adult life had been devoted to the communist movement, and though he still believed in its ideals, his experience with the party had left him deeply disappointed. Yet he had a grace about this period of his life: "I learned a good many things and met many great people. You cannot live in regret; you did what you did to the best of your ability at the time." His second career earned him honors and awards as an editor, and when he was at the age when most people were winding down he began to paint. In his eighties, his paintings were exhibited, and even the gallery owners were surprised when they all sold, and merited another show, and another.

The last time we met, he sat on a small park bench, his hands folded in his lap. "Sometimes I talk to people who are in their forties or fifties, and they are already talking as if their life were almost over. But I want to tell them: Look, you have only been an adult for twenty or twenty-five years. It is not very much time to figure life out. And if you live to be my age, you may have another entire adult lifetime or maybe two before you die. So don't give up on yourself."

Recall that Elsa, in her seventies, had a very difficult childhood growing up in Germany during World War II. She told me that when she looks at pictures of herself as a child, she finds herself wanting to offer that child the perspective she has gained so many years later. "I look so sad in every picture, never smiling. Sometimes I want to talk to that child, to tell her to hold on and have faith because her dreams will come true, and she will find happiness. And I want to say that to every person who hears about these interviews, that if you hold on, if you keep growing, you will find your dreams and make a difference while you are here."

It is my hope that each person who reads this book will experience the same grace and perspective that these wise people offered me. Stop judging the life you have lived and get on with the life you still may live. Whatever mistakes you have made and no matter how many regrets may litter your past, plant a new tree today. Begin to live the secrets now or simply live them more deeply. This is what the wise elders wanted me to know.

how this book changed me

Over the last year, whenever I told someone about this project, about the200 conversations with people who had lived a long life and found wisdom, I was often asked "how did those conversations change you?" It is a great question, and I want to share the answer with you.

As I mentioned in the prologue, three of us conducted these interviews, I and two colleagues, Olivia McIvor and Leslie Knight. The bulk of the interviews, just over 200, were conducted by Olivia and me. Both of us are in our late forties. At times, it was like sitting with our own grandmothers or grandfathers but with a kind of openness we often miss with those closest to us. The people we interviewed told us the stories of their lives. Sometimes they told us about painful memories and about deep regrets; other times they told us about joyous moments.

Sometimes I was in tears as people told me about moments of great loss or hurt. Other times I was inspired and moved. There were many times when I did not want the interview to end because I felt a deep sense of peace listening to the voice of a particularly wise person. Once I even cried when the interview was over, because I felt I was letting go of something that would never come again, a momentary experience of bliss caught up in the story of another human being's life.

Even while the interviews were still in process, I began to find myself changing in small ways. As I went about my daily activities, an image or a story would come into my mind. For example, a 93-year-old man told me about how he cries each time he sees a sunset or a ballet, not only because he was getting to experience it but because he never knows when it will be his last. In the month that followed that conversation, I found myself savoring particular moments with a much deeper sense of attentiveness. Suddenly, I was aware that no matter what our age, we never know when we will see our last sunset, and as I began to live my days with that deeper attentiveness, suddenly the sunsets seemed to be more colorful, and it somehow seemed that the moments of joy began to increase.

Over time, it became a common occurrence for me to think of particular words and phrases as I went about my life. The images of these people and the things they said kept resonating. When I was walking and grumbling, I would think of the man who took gratitude walks. When I woke up in the morning, I started saying thank you for another day just as Joel had advised me. When I met a stranger, I would recall stories from people who found out years later what a difference they had made in a stranger's life and suddenly find myself being kinder. Whenever I found myself judging my life, I would think of how many people had told me to live instead of judging, and whenever I found myself content, I remembered a man who told me to remember that "happiness is all in your head."

One of the people I interviewed told me about an experience he had as a young man working in a factory. A late–middle-aged man who worked alongside him had lost half an arm in an industrial accident. Every day he would raise his wooden arm and implore Bill to get an education lest he turn out like him. "Many years later I can still see him sitting there imploring me not to make the same mistakes he had made. I have often thought of him sitting there, kind of like Captain Hook, holding up his wooden arm with the claw, telling me to be careful." Since the interviews I have often felt that way, as if these people were holding up the truths they shared with me and asking me to follow.

The interviews changed my view of death as well as life. We don't talk very openly about death in our society. It surrounds us all our life, but we pretend it is not there, as if talking about death might summon its untimely arrival or that by ignoring it we can avoid it. In these interviews, I found myself talking to people about dying in an honest and often intimate way. Day after day, I would ask this question without hesitation or even the appearance of apology: "Now that you are older, how are you feeling about death, *not death in the abstract*, but *your death?*"

These people taught me that a person who lives wisely will not be afraid to die. Afraid of pain perhaps, afraid of becoming a burden to others, yes, but happy people are not afraid to die. Many times now when I think about my own death, I find I can access the peace I heard day after day in the voices of these people who calmly told me: "I have lived well and when I die I will be ready." When we have lived, we can die. I also learned that until we accept that death is a part of life, we are not ready to embrace life. Death is both our greatest teacher and a friend in disguise. When we recognize that our time is limited, only then will we live with the urgency required to discover what really matters. Living now as if today's might be my last sunset, I found myself being more present.

Most of all, these interviews reminded me of some things

that I already knew but that can be forgotten in the distracted busy-ness of a modern life. They reminded me to stop and really enjoy life, to be a more loving person, to make sure I leave no regrets, to be true to my self, and to know that it is by giving that I become a part of something larger than I am.

One of the most inspiring interviews I conducted was with Don. My interview with him lasted over two hours, and when it was finished I found myself welling up with tears. At first I had no idea of the source of those tears, but then I realized that for those two hours I had known I was in the presence of wisdom, of something ancient. For two hours, I was a witness to the secrets of what it means to be human, and I did not want to let the experience go. Again and again, I came up with another question, extending our time together. Finally I had no choice but to end the interview.

For many months thereafter I traded e-mails with Don. Once we had even arranged to meet for dinner near his home in Baltimore, but my business trip was postponed. The next time I am in Baltimore, I e-mailed him, we will meet for sure. Several times I said I would call him but never quite got around to it during my busy days. Four days before my next trip to Baltimore, an e-mail arrived in my inbox with the terse subject line: FW-Thought You Might Want to Know the Passing of Don Klein. I have never had such an emotional reaction to the thought of opening an e-mail. For hours I refused to open it, somehow believing that it would not be real unless I read it.

There were so many things I wanted to ask Don, things I still wanted to know. I wanted to have that feeling again of being in the presence of wisdom. Most of all, I wanted to tell him that his words and the words of others had changed me and that the book would change the lives of still others. The words of another one of my favorite interviewees rang in my ears: "Don't count on cramming—if something is important to you, do it now." As I stared at the e-mail, those words became more than a nice saying, and grief welled up in me. The thought that I would never get to speak with Don again overwhelmed me.

Opening the e-mail, I found a letter from his son. In it he described the last few weeks of his father's life. His life had ended the way he had lived his 83 years. He had just taken a cross-Atlantic cruise with his brother and was in California giving a talk on his great passion, which was love. On his way back to his seat he collapsed. Efforts to revive him failed. He died in the arms of one of his closest friends.

In my office I listened to the recording of his interview. He said: "I have had a heart problem for almost 20 years now and had a heart failure episode. The rescue squad came and revived me. I did not see a white light, but I felt very much at peace; I knew it was going to be fine. Since then I have had no fear of death. My life has been a great gift.When I go, I will be ready." Through tears, I smiled. I knew he had died in peace; he had discovered and lived the five secrets.

I listened as he talked about his wife of 56 years, whom he had seen across the dance floor in college, and of how he overcame his shyness and how that small risk changed his life. When I asked him if he still felt her presence he said: "Oh yes, she has been gone now for six years, but every day I feel her presence. When love touches you it never dies."

Leaning back in my chair, I closed my eyes, and the feeling of being in the presence of wisdom returned. The love of these several hundred people had touched me deeply, and they would walk with me for the rest of my life.

the secret to life
in one sentence or less

We asked the people we interviewed to share with us, in one sentence or less, the secret to a fulfilling and happy life. We invited them to share their secret with those younger than themselves. In some cases, they went over the one-sentence limit, but putting a lifetime in one sentence isn't easy.

Here are some selected secrets to life:

There are ten-minute funeral lines and ten-hour funeral lines. Live your life so that when you die people will want to stay and tell stories about the kind of life you lived and how you touched them.
    —Ken Krambeer, town barber, 64

Recognize that you are born with the capacity to be in the world and not dependent on the circumstance in which you find yourself; don't take yourself seriously, don't get trapped by the ideas in your head; they are not the same as the reality.
    —Donald Klein, psychologist and author, 84

Don't count on cramming. I always told my students—if you follow your heart, leave a legacy, and focus on what matters, it will be ok.
    —George Beer, physicist, retired professor, 71

Love someone deeply and be loved by someone deeply; be passionate about yourself and your curiosity and exploration and really GO FOR IT.
    —William Hawfield, 64

In order to find a more purposeful life you must let go of what society and people think of you and look inside yourself through some discipline—prayer, meditation—to find out what matters most to you and pursue it.
    —James Autry, poet and author, 73

If you are unhappy, get busy doing something for someone else. If you concentrate on yourself you will be unhappy, but if you focus on helping others you will find happiness. Happiness comes from serving and loving.
    —Juana Bordas, author, 64

Banish the word "boredom" from your vocabulary, and wherever you are make the most of that moment because you won't get it back.
    —Max Wyman, 65

Kneel down and kiss the earth, be thankful that you exist, love yourself and those around you, and enjoy the hell out of being alive.
    —Craig Neal, 60

Remember you are part of something larger than yourself.
     —**Antony Holland, actor, 86**

Find your passion and pursue it.
     —**Lea Williams, author and educator, 58**

Find something you love doing and make it your career.
     —**Paul Hersey, author, 76**

My mother told me "to thine ownself be true"—it is important advice and will pay huge dividends if you learn what is true for yourself—be true to what matters to you and this requires reflection and you can't think while watching *The Simpsons.*
     —**Jim Scott, real estate broker, 60**

The legacy you leave is the life you lead. We lead our lives daily, and we leave a legacy daily—not some grand plan, what we do each and every day, all the little decisions, because we never know what impact things will have or when you might have an impact.
     —**Jim Kouzes, author, 61**

Learn to love people, because if you do, it will carry you to all kinds of places—see the good in other people always.
     —**John Boyd, painter, almost 94**

I cannot give one sentence of advice to others because first I would have to know them, so I say know yourself and know what you want to create in your life and hold that in front of yourself ALWAYS.
     —**Elsa Neuner, 72**

Eat healthy, be physically active, invest your energy in making wherever you are a more just and happy community.
   —William Gorden, professor of communication, activist, 77

Always see the good in people, and you won't get hurt because everybody has so much goodness in them. Don't envy other people, because you have different gifts and blessings.
   —Eileen Lindesay, 78

Learn to step out of the boat more.
   —Don, 78

Live everyday for what it is, don't worry about what will happen, the next day will take care of itself, what will be will be, learn to accept and wait for the next day to happen.
   —Esther, 89

Never dwell on the negative in your life, bad things happen all the time, even in bad situations look for the good and you will find it.
   —Rufus Riggs, 63

Live your passion and be of service to others.
   —Laura Lowe, 61

Get an education, find out who you are, where you came from and where you want to go, and don't forget who you are.
   —Ralph Dick, native chief, 66

You need to learn who you are inside, figure out what your feelings are, understand that; the key to self-knowledge. If you know who you are, then you are grounded throughout life. If everything is a mystery to you, then you are going to be in trouble.
    —Mark Sherkow, 60

Don't draw the curtain too soon; there is always an encore or fourth act.
    —Joci James, 79

Pick a career that you enjoy and [gives you] a sense of accomplishment. It's not how many dollars you put in your jeans. The money can disappear quickly, but the sense of accomplishment doesn't. You go to bed with it at night and you sleep like a baby.
    —Gordon Fuerst, 71

Listen to the voices inside of you, they will tell you what is right and what is wrong, they will bring you happiness and peace; if you don't listen to them they can create anxiety, discontentment, and unhappiness.
    —Bert Wilson, 63

Remember the Lord God has His eye on you and His hand on your shoulder.
    —Robin Brians, 67

Know thy self and have the courage to follow that.
    —Clive Martin, 65

Be kind to yourself and to others; you can't go wrong that way.
—**Mary, 87**

Choose to have a happy life. If you want to focus on what is wrong, then so be it. Or you can focus on the lily in the front yard that opened today and you get to see it today, it's what you focus on that counts.
—**Tony, 66**

Be nice to everyone, and people will love you when you grow up.
—**Jay Jacobson, 65**

When I was coaching my kids, which I did all of them, I said this so often they could repeat it back to me—play hard, be a good sport and have fun: Throw yourself into it, be honest, a fair player, and don't take life or yourself too seriously. I'd rather win than lose, but playing the game is what matters.
—**Jack Lowe, business owner, 67**

Follow your heart and become the person you want to be in the world.
—**Bob Peart, biologist and activist, 59**

Each person has a very specific purpose; you're given all the tools you need.
—**Tom McCallum, White Standing Buffalo, 60**

Have the discipline to listen to your heart, and then have the courage to follow.
—**Ron Polack, healer of energies, 72**

Have as much fun, joy, and pleasure as you can while causing no harm to others.
   —Lee Pulos, psychologist, 78

Be all of yourself; listen like you love that person, get a vision of your future that is authentic to yourself that will make a difference in the world, and honor every moment you are alive.
   —Joel Barker, author and futurist, 62

Be as curious and respectful of other people as you can, be inventive about how to bring more excitement into your interactions—be out there.
   —Susan Samuels-Drake, 68

Find your path and be true to it.
   —William Bridges, author, 73

Pay your bills! Don't make money your goal; mange your money, choose a job that you're going to enjoy, 'cuz you're going to spend a lot of time doing it.
   —May, 72

Stay busy; never be bored; always find five more things to do.
   —Lucy, nurse, 101

Enjoy every day; make friends; don't squabble.
   —Alice Reid, 97

Learn all you can, listen to the best advisors that you can, and pray to God to lead you.
   —Father John Edward Brown, Catholic priest, 89

When I was in school I said to my woodwork teacher that what I was working on was "good enough," and he told me only perfect is good enough and good enough is not perfect.
  —**Frank, 82**

To thyself be true, do what is right for you, and be your own person, do what makes your heart sing.
  —**Reverend Farolyn Mann, 67**

Dive in with both feet, roll up your sleeves and get messy, dare to live, dare to love, dare to connect.
  —**Ann Britt, 67**

Love what you do and do what you love.
  —**Darlene Burcham, 62**

Live by the golden rule: treat everyone the way you want to be treated.
  —**Wayne Huffman, 68**

Believe in yourself, we all have wonderful gifts.
  —**Jacqueline Gould, 60**

Seek to learn from the past, enjoy the present, and make way for a better future.
  —**Mary Ruth Snyder, 79**

Be strong, be kind, and be loving to your fellow man.
  —**Elizabeth, 85**

Love yourself and the rest will follow.
  —**Jeannie Runnalls, 57**

Do not be ruled by fear.
        —**Felisa Cheng, 65**

Work as hard as you can, and give your all to what you are doing; strive to do the best. Set your goals high; if you set them
too low you will go below that mark.
        —**Muriel Douglas, 72**

Do good if you can to every person you meet, but always do
no harm.
        —**Bansi Gandhi, 63**

Have a deep respect for yourself and others. Do not do any
harm to others, and accept others as they are.
        —**Juliana Kratz, 76**

Keep your vision and keep focused. Trust in yourself and keep
going toward your goal; you will get there, you might not know
how, but you will.
        —**Dyane Lynch, 63**

Don't sweat the small stuff.
        —**John Smith, 82**

interviewing your own wise elders

In some ways, my journey of writing this book represented an unfinished personal quest. Many of the most important mentors in my life died before I got to talk to them about their lives and what they had learned. I wish I had had the chance to ask them the questions we asked the people we interviewed for this book.

Many of the people we talked to were recommended by someone very close to them, often a son or a daughter. One of the most poignant moments in the project occurred after a son had suggested that we interview his father for the book. He told us that his father was wise and had discovered meaning in life. Obviously, the son felt his father had something important to pass on to others. Unfortunately, while we were arranging his interview, he died. My team felt a deep sadness that we had not interviewed him in time. His wisdom would not be shared, at least not in this book.

It got us to thinking that many of those who read this book will know an older person who has found meaning in life, whose wisdom they might want to capture before the person dies—either to share with family members or simply to hear for themselves. So, we decided to share with you the questions we asked our interviewees, in the hope that this might be the beginning of a larger conversation, in which each of us seeks the wisdom of others.

As I mentioned in the prologue, when we interviewed the wise elders, pauses often occurred between our questions and their answers. In these moments, I often asked myself the same questions. I tried to imagine being the age of the person I was interviewing and wondered how I would answer. So, I hope that, in addition to using these questions to interview others, each of you will ask yourself these questions as well.

1. Pretend you are at a dinner party, and everyone is sitting in a circle. The host invites each person to take just a few minutes to describe the life he or she has lived. If you were at the party and you wanted people to know as much about your life as possible in those few minutes, what would you say? Describe the life you have lived thus far.

2. What has brought you the greatest sense of meaning and purpose in life? Why does it matter that you were alive?

3. What brought you/brings you the most happiness in life, the greatest joy moment to moment?

4. Tell me about a few of the major "crossroads" moments in your life, times when you went in one direction or another and it made a large difference in terms of how your life turned out?

5. What is the best advice you ever got from someone else about life? Did you take that advice? How have you used it during your life?

6. What do you wish you had learned sooner? If you could go back to when you were a young adult and have a conversation with yourself, and you knew you would listen, what would you tell that younger person about life?

7. What is the role that spirituality has played in your life?

8. What is the greatest fear at the end of life?

9. Now that you are older, how do you feel about your mortality, about death? Not death in the abstract but your death? Are you afraid of dying?

10. What role have spirituality and religion played in your life? What have you concluded about "God"?

11. Fill in this sentence, I wish I had . . .

12. Now that you have lived most of your life, what are you certain or almost certain matters a great deal if a person wants to find happiness and live a fulfilling life?

13. Now that you have lived most of your life, what are you certain or almost certain does not matter very much in finding a happy life? What do you wish you had paid less attention to?

14. If you could give only one sentence of advice to those younger than you on finding a happy and meaningful life, what one sentence would you pass on?

list of interviewees

The following interviewees agreed to have their names appear in the book. We thank these people for sharing their wisdom. To those who did not want their names published or who died before we could get their permission, we also give thanks.

Walburga Ahlquist
Abu al-Basri
Fateema al-Basri
James Autry
Ann Ayres

Pravin Barinder
Joel Barker
George Beer
Emily Bell
Juana Bordas
John Boyd
Robin Brians
William Bridges

Ann Britt
Ammod Briyani
Father John Edward Brown
Darlene Burcham
Ron Butler

Pat Campbell
Olive Charnell
Felisa Cheng
Sylvia Cust
Amy Damoni
Robert Davies
Ralph Dick
Muriel (Jamie) Douglas

Susan Samuels Drake
June Dyer

Gerry Ellery
Immanuel Ephraim

Gordon Fuerst
E. Margaret Fulton

Bansi Gandhi
Harvey Gold
Maggie Goldman
William Gorden
Jacqueline Gould
David Gouthro

William Hawfield
Orville Hendersen
Pablo Herrera
Paul Hersey
Antony Holland
Lauretta Howard
Wayne Huffman

Abdullah ibn Abbas

Lamar Jackson
Jay Jacobson
Joci James
Evelyn Jones

Sr. Elizabeth Kelliher
Loretta Keys
Donald Klein
Ada Knight
Ronald Komas
Jim Kouzes

Ken Krambeer
Juliana Kratz

Jacob Leider
Lucie Liebman
Eileen Brigid Lindesay
George Littlemore
Martha Lofendale
Dan London
Jack Lowe
Laura Lowe
Dyane Lynch

Gordon Mains
Reverend Farolyn Mann
Clive Martin
Tom McCallum
Carlos Montana

Craig Neal
Juanita Neal
Elsa Neuner
Joyce Nolin
Jesse Nyquist

Derek O'Toole

Irene Parisi
Bob Peart
Dick Pieper
Ronald Polack
Lee Pulos

Alice Reid
Rufus Riggs
Felicia Riley
Jeannie Runnalls

Murray Running

John Sandeen
Jim Scott
Mark Sherkow
John (Jack) Smith
Lynn Smith
Mary Ruth Snyder
Joel Solomon
Jerry Spinarski

May Taylor
Patricia Thomas

Tom Waddill
Harvey Walker
Bryan Wall
Bucky Walters
Esther Watkins
Lea Williams
Bert Wilson
Robert Wong
Max Wyman

index

about the author

Dr. John Izzo

An award-winning writer and author, corporate culture crusader, and global sustainability advocate, John B. Izzo, Ph.D., has devoted his life and career to facilitating deeper conversations about personal values, work culture, life-fulfillment, leadership responsibility, and the true definition of "success." Since age 12, John Izzo wanted to do his part to influence and inspire people. He has worked with thousands of leaders, professionals, and front-line colleagues to foster workplaces of excellence, purpose, learning, and renewal. He has led retreats on creating sustainability, being a better leader, and finding fulfillment in work and life. And he has interviewed and stayed in touch with thousands of individuals to ensure the pulse of people's needs is palpable and understood. His beliefs, wisdom, and experience have helped people discover practical ways to create engaged workplaces and intentional, positive lives.

Izzo obtained his Bachelor of Sociology from Hofstra University in 1978 then completed dual Masters degree programs (from McCormick Divinity School in Theology, simultaneously attending the University of Chicago to complete a Masters in Organizational Psychology). Izzo went on to earn his Ph.D. in Organizational Communication from Kent State University. He has served on the faculty of three major universities and is the past board chair of both the Sierra Club and the Canadian Parks and Wilderness Society.

Dr. Izzo has shared platforms around the world with politicians, environmentalists, corporate icons, foundation heads and movie magnates like Ken Blanchard, Bill Clinton, David Suzuki, Oprah Winfrey, Peter Mansbridge, Jane Fonda, and Dr. Brian Little, and he is asked to speak to over 100 audiences each year. He has authored and published over 600 articles, and is the author of three national best-selling books: *Second Innocence, Values Shift,* and *Awakening Corporate Soul. Fast Company,* CNN, Wisdom Network, Canada–AM, ABC *World News, Working Woman,* the *Wall Street Journal, McLean's* Magazine and *INC* Magazine have featured the research and opinions of John Izzo, and he is also a frequent contributor to the *Globe and Mail* as well as *Association Management* Magazine.

In 2007, The Biography Channel and Dr. Izzo filmed a five-part series titled "The Five Things You Must Discover Before You Die." This series is currently airing on The Biography Channel in Canada as well as PBS in the United States.

Born and raised on the East Coast of the United States, Dr. Izzo now lives with his wife and children in the mountains outside Vancouver, Canada. For more information on Dr. John Izzo and his colleagues visit

www.drjohnizzo.com
http://www.drjohnizzo.com/
or
www.theizzogroup.com
http://www.theizzogroup.com/

the five secrets DVD series
the show that inspired the book

This book was based on Dr. John Izzo's five-part television series "The Five Things You Must Discover Before You Die," airing on The Biography Channel in Canada and PBS in the United States. This television series brings to life the people and interviews you read about in this book and allows you to hear Dr. Izzo talk about his experiences in his research to discover the five secrets.

The series features Dr. Izzo speaking for five hours before a live audience as well as interview clips from actual interviews with some of these "wise elders." Dr. Izzo will touch your heart and give you practical ways to make the Five Secrets become reality in your life. Dr. Izzo offers guidance and support as we all try to experience the most we can in the time we have here. It delves into the lives of wise people aged 65–105 as well. Meet Elsa, John, Ron, Max, and many more of the wise people you read about in this book as this DVD series inspires you with their personal stories.

John Izzo talks to us about focusing our lives on the things that leave no regrets. The breadth of experience and knowledge this gentleman's life offers us all is shown in this heartwarming and inspiring five-part series.

If you enjoyed this book, this DVD series has more stories, more words from John Izzo, and will bring the book to life in a heartwarming experience you won't want to miss. To order: www.drjohnizzo.com or www.fairwinds-press.com

 *Second Innocence* is about rediscovering the wonder and joys of life at any age. Based on his own unique experiences—the death of his father, a rowing trip with his grandfather, his first real job, first love, a family suicide, teachers he remembers for their unique courage, and his experiences as a leader, lover, parent, and friend—John's stories will encourage you to reconnect with and learn from your own life stories. Izzo's compelling narrative, in which he tackles four key areas of human experience (daily life, work, love, and faith), will lead you to new perspectives on your own life and provide thought-provoking insights for reclaiming the innocence, idealism, and wonder that we often associate with youth.

$15.95, paperback, 208 pages, ISBN 978-1-57675-263-0

working with dr. izzo

Dr. John Izzo speaks on topics related to life, leadership, spirituality and responsibility. His appearance schedule is available on his web site.

To inquire further about Dr. Izzo's availability to speak at your upcoming event, please inquire at: info@drjohnizzo.com.

Contact information:
Office (604) 913-0649
Fax (604) 913-0648

e-mail: info@drjohnizzo.com

Web site: www.drjohnizzo.com
or
www.theizzogroup.com

about berrett-koehler publishers

Berrett-Koehler is an independent publisher dedicated to an ambitious mission: Creating a World that Works for All.

We believe that to truly create a better world, action is needed at all levels—individual, organizational, and societal. At the individual level, our publications help people align their lives with their values and with their aspirations for a better world. At the organizational level, our publications promote progressive leadership and management practices, socially responsible approaches to business, and humane and effective organizations. At the societal level, our publications advance social and economic justice, shared prosperity, sustainability, and new solutions to national and global issues.

A major theme of our publications is "Opening Up New Space." They challenge conventional thinking, introduce new ideas, and foster positive change. Their common quest is changing the underlying beliefs, mindsets, and structures that keep generating the same cycles of problems, no matter who our leaders are or what improvement programs we adopt.

We strive to practice what we preach—to operate our publishing company in line with the ideas in our books. At the core of our approach is *stewardship*, which we define as a deep sense of responsibility to administer the company for the benefit of all of our "stakeholder" groups: authors, customers, employees, investors, service providers, and the communities and environment around us.

We are grateful to the thousands of readers, authors, and other friends of the company who consider themselves to be part of the "BK Community." We hope that you, too, will join us in our mission.

a bk life book

This book is part of our BK Life series. BK Life books change people's lives. They help individuals improve their lives in ways that are beneficial for the families, organizations, communities, nations, and world in which they live and work. To find out more, visit www.bk-life.com

be connected

visit our website

Go to www.bkconnection.com to read exclusive previews
and excerpts of new books, find detailed information on all
Berrett-Koehler titles and authors, browse subject-area libraries
of books, and get special discounts.

subscribe to our free e-newsletter

Be the first to hear about new publications, special discount
offers, exclusive articles, news about bestsellers, and more!
Get on the list for our free e-newsletter by going to www.
bkconnection.com

get quantity discounts

Berrett-Koehler books are available at quantity discounts
for orders of ten or more copies. Please call us toll-free at
(800) 929-2929 or e-mail us at bkp.orders@aidcvt.com

host a reading group

For tips on how to form and carry on a book reading group
in your workplace or community, see our website at www.
bkconnection.com

join the bk community

Thousands of readers of our books have become part of the
"BK Community" by participating in events featuring our
authors, reviewing draft manuscripts of forthcoming books,
spreading the word about their favorite books, and support-
ing our publishing program in other ways. If you would like to
join the BK Community, please contact us at bkcommunity@
bkpub.com.